DBT Workbook For Teens

A Complete Dialectical Behavior Therapy Toolkit

Essential Coping Skills and Practical Activities
To Help Teenagers & Adolescents Manage
Stress, Anxiety, ADHD, Phobias & More

By Barrett Huang

https://barretthuang.com/

© Copyright 2022 by Barrett Huang. All rights reserved.

This book contains information that is as accurate and reliable as possible. Regardless, purchasing this book constitutes agreement that both the publisher and the author of this book are in no way experts on the topics discussed and that any comments or suggestions made herein are solely for educational purposes. The information provided is not intended as a substitute for professional medical advice, diagnosis, or treatment. Always consult a professional before taking any action advised herein.

This declaration is deemed fair and valid by both the American Bar Association and the Committee of Publishers Association and is legally binding throughout the United States.

Furthermore, the transmission, duplication, or reproduction of any of the following work, including specific information, will be considered illegal, whether it is done electronically or in print. This extends to creating a secondary or tertiary copy of the work or a recorded copy and is only allowed with express written consent from the publisher. All additional rights reserved.

The information in the following pages is broadly considered a truthful and accurate account of facts. Any inattention, use, or misuse of the information in question by the reader will render any resulting actions solely under their purview. There are no scenarios in which the publisher or the original author of this work can be deemed liable for any hardship or damages that may occur after undertaking the information described herein.

Additionally, the information in the following pages is intended only for informational purposes and should thus be thought of as universal. It is presented without assurance regarding its prolonged validity or interim quality as befitting its nature. Trademarks mentioned are done without written consent and should not be considered an endorsement from the trademark holder.

Table of Contents

Introduction

"Our wounds are often the openings into the best and most beautiful parts of us."
— David Richo

When young adults are exposed to an environment of chaos and uncertainty, they can easily switch to a survival mode of living instead of thriving.

Growing up, my father was a hoarder, and my mother lived with undiagnosed anxiety. I felt undeniably anxious and confused as a child with emotionally absent parents. Nothing was 'stable' in my world.

Sadly, these chaotic internal feelings and unrest I experienced as a kid negatively influenced my everyday behavior and approach to life.

For example, I was always anticipating bad things to happen at every corner. What started as 'habits' or 'mannerisms' soon spiraled into full-blown Obsessive-Compulsive Disorder (OCD).

One of my *obsessions* was to avoid stepping on cracks on the pavement. My every step needed to land perfectly. Otherwise, my day was doomed. Can you imagine walking this way for years?!?

One of my *compulsions* revolved around 'checking'. I was constantly double-checking all the door locks to ensure I hadn't left anything unattended that may lead to a disaster.

So I would check the door lock, go away and do something, doubt myself if I had checked it, go back to the door, check the lock again, move away, and after a few hours... Can you imagine living like this every single day?!?

Not surprisingly, this constant fear and worry molded me into an adult with not just OCD but Generalized Anxiety Disorder (GAD) too.

Did I get better? Luckily, I did.

Seeking help for my disorders from professionals in the mental health field and using prescribed anti-anxiety medication made me into the well-adjusted person I am today.

But I will be 100% honest with you. Anxiety never truly goes away. It's an integral part of human emotions and feelings. Anxiety is a 'warning sign'. For example, if you're anxious about something (e.g., how you're doing at school), then maybe you should spend time thinking about it; perhaps you need to make changes to get better grades. It's when anxiety becomes paralyzing and draining to the point that it gets in the way of leading a normal life—that's when it is unhealthy.

And I know it is a struggle. Even today, I still sometimes think I need to be on my toes and prepare for some impending doom.

However, with effective techniques and support, I manage it well. These emotions no longer take over my life.

So you can say that the inspiration behind writing this DBT-focused book for young adults and teens emerged from my journey since it changed my life. I have a B.A. in Psychology and completed the DBT Skills certificate course by Dr. Marsha Linehan. However, I'd like to emphasize that this book strongly draws from my personal experiences with OCD, GAD, and depression and how DBT helped me cope with these mental issues. This book talks about mental health issues other than those I've had because I want to help young adults who are going through these problems and show how DBT can be used in these situations.

I have worked with both Cognitive Behavior Therapy (CBT) and Dialectic Behavior Therapy (DBT). While they are both useful approaches, I strongly believe that every individual is unique, and this book is for individuals who have already tried CBT and other tools but didn't find them effective.

The book is laid out in a user-friendly manner to make navigating through it easier for adolescents. A quick rundown of mental health disorders among teens is presented in Chapter 1. This is soon followed by the basics of DBT in Chapter 2. The following chapters will discuss these common mental health issues in more detail AND provide relevant DBT exercises to help young adults cope and address them.

> *"Life is determined to introduce you to your true self. Be kind."*
> **–Richelle E. Goodrich**

I strongly believe that the key to living a fulfilling life is finding your *authentic self* and embracing it. Sadly, it is usually during our adolescent years when we lose our sense of self while struggling with mental health challenges.

According to the World Health Organization (WHO), the general unfortunate statistic is that globally, *1 in every 7 young adults (10- to 19-year-olds) has a mental health disorder*[1], which often becomes lifelong.

I sincerely hope that this book helps to lower that statistic.

My goal is to help the youth discover DBT as a highly effective tool to cope with mental health challenges. DBT enabled me to live a fulfilling life. And I hope it does the same for you.

I am grateful to you for trusting me
by being here.

In my experience, this journey is not linear.
There will be a lot of ups and downs...
but I promise that it is a rewarding one.

I also want you all to know that you are not
alone in fighting your battles. I experienced it,
and millions of other adolescents are going
through it now.

But know that there is help available to you.

This book is one of them. May it become a
guiding source for you while you embark on
your path of healing.

Chapter 1: What Is Happening to Me?

"Knowing yourself is the beginning of all wisdom."
- Aristotle

It is no surprise that young adults are becoming more stressed daily. Increased exposure to social media, the internet, and technology have greatly connected us. But it has also resulted in increased expectations to succeed in ways previous generations did not endure.

About 75% of Gen Z aged between 15 and 21 struggle with mental health challenges.[2] Multiple factors have contributed to reaching this number, including, but not limited to, dysfunctional family dynamics, traumatic experiences, and, as mentioned, technology.

Since I have a father who's a hoarder and a mother with undiagnosed anxiety, growing up in a household with emotionally absent parents made me feel alone and isolated in this big world. The restless environment I was raised in shaped me into an adult with mental health issues.

I went to school with approximately 5000 other students during my teen years. However, I never felt comfortable enough to be friends with any of them. The void I felt made me believe that I didn't deserve to be loved. (I know now that that's not true, but it wasn't what I believed then.)

I also remember getting extremely nervous during social situations. Just talking to someone would drive me to start fumbling with my thumbs, picking at my nails, and the words would mumble out of my mouth, leaving me so frustrated!

I truly was not aware of what was happening to me. And because I didn't understand the reason for my struggles, I simply couldn't cope. I withdrew more and more from everything and from everyone.

Now, I know I was never taught enough vocabulary to translate my thoughts, emotions, and struggles into words. I was never given the tools I needed to figure out what my mind was struggling with.

Back then, I would just be a ball of frustration and loneliness. Today, whenever I look back, I feel empathy for my younger self.

So this chapter is dedicated to helping you understand yourself and the struggles you're going through.

The following briefly explains the leading common mental health disorders among young adults. You will likely see yourself in one or more of these situations. And when you do, don't be afraid or ashamed. It's the first step to healing.

Anxiety, Stress, and Worry

It's your first day at school, and you're a nervous wreck. Your mouth is dry; your heart feels like it's trying to hammer its way out of your chest, and you have this sinking feeling in your stomach. A part of you knows you shouldn't feel like this; it is irrational, but you can't help it. In fact, you feel like you're spiraling out of control. This is anxiety.

Anxiety can also show up as the following symptoms:

- Disturbed sleep pattern.
- Difficulty concentrating.
- Sweating.
- Dizziness.
- Numbness.
- Distress.

You can't erase anxiety from your life. Truth be told, anxiety is a natural response of the body when exposed to a stressful situation or when something threatening is perceived. It is an exaggerated fear about what is to come. When you start feeling anxious, your body becomes alert and looks for possible stressors or signs of danger.

Anxiety can be caused by several genetic and environmental factors. But for many adolescents today, much anxiety comes from social media.

Social media can be fun. But the flip side is that access to others' lives makes us compare our lives to theirs. Someone at school has a lot of parties and friends? You may get envious. I know I did.

Someone has a new mobile phone? New clothes? If you cannot afford this, you may think their lives are 'more', while yours is 'less'. I know I felt this way.

I grew up with this anxiety. Even though I have a thriving business now, I sometimes feel anxious to hustle more, thinking that achieving more will automatically improve my life.

It also doesn't help that we have 24/7 access to news fueled by fear, hate, and division. As I got older, I made a deliberate decision to STOP watching the news because it was causing more anxiety in my life.

It was during my stay in Asia that the reality of things dawned upon me.

I experienced a lot of extreme poverty around me in Bangkok, Manila, and China. Even though the locals had meager wages and limited resources, they appeared happy and content with their lives. How can that be?!?

Their unwavering smiles compelled me to reflect deeply, and eventually, I realized how fortunate I was. Heck, compared to them, I had won the lottery!

I grew up in a first-world country (Canada) and had a loving family and a warm place to come back home every night. If these locals could survive in what I viewed as extremely difficult living conditions, then what was I worried about?

And then I had that light-bulb moment: **my anxiety was actually the thing that was stopping me from living in the moment and enjoying life**.

And so, the healing journey began. I took up therapy and put my attention on myself.

ADHD / ADD

ADHD (Attention Deficit Hyperactivity Disorder) is a common neurodevelopmental disorder that usually manifests in childhood but can also last into adulthood. It is further divided into three categories: *inattentive*, *hyperactive*, and *mixed*.

Children with inattentive ADHD struggle with focus; they find it difficult to maintain attention for longer periods. Memory loss, disorganization, and difficulty understanding and following instructions are prevalent problems as well. Kids with ADHD are easily sidetracked and prone to making blunders that appear thoughtless.

Hyperactive ADHD involves an urge to constantly move. This need for movement includes fidgeting, squirming, and running around. People with this type of ADHD have low self-control, which is often seen in their communication skills. For example, they tend to cut off others, talk rapidly, and yell without much thought.

Mixed ADHD is when someone shows both inattentive and hyperactive ADHD symptoms.

ADD (Attention Deficit Disorder) is an outdated term for inattentive ADHD. Some people still use ADD as it excludes the hyperactivity part altogether. It has a wide range of symptoms which includes:

- Impulsive behavior.
- Trouble multitasking.
- Frustration.
- Excessive activeness or restlessness.
- Lack of focus.
- Mood swings.
- Trouble understanding.

Phobias

A phobia is a strong, unrealistic fear of any object, person, activity, animal, or situation. When someone has a phobia of something, they try to stay away from it as much as possible. And if they ever have to face their fear, they do so with a lot of stress and worry.

A phobia can be about something very specific, like spiders. On the other hand, a phobia can cover a wider range of things, like a fear of heights; any height can be in the range. For example, this fear can be brought on by being at the top of a 16-story building or just looking out of a first-floor window.

A phobia can make it hard to do normal things. In extreme cases, it can lead to paralyzation (i.e., paralyzed by fear), anxiety, and depression. A phobia can also cause a panic attack, which can manifest as sweating, hot flashes or chills, a feeling of choking, nausea, increased heart rate, and problems with the bladder.

PTSD & Panic Disorders

When someone goes through something bad like intense fear or a traumatic event, it can have an effect that lasts a long time. This is called Post-Traumatic Stress Disorder (PTSD).

You don't have to be directly involved in the traumatic event to suffer from PTSD. It can be caused by simply seeing something terrible, like a car accident, a terrorist attack, or something tragic that happened at your school.

PTSD can make it hard to sleep or focus. They can cause nightmares, night terrors (i.e., a sleep disorder that causes feelings of panic), make you overly alert, and bring on panic attacks. When these panic attacks get too bad, they can become panic disorders, which can manifest as intense shaking and troubled breathing.

OCD & Compulsive Behaviors

OCD (Obsessive-Compulsive Disorder) is another common mental illness in the modern world. It involves having repeated, unwanted, and irrational thoughts (*obsessions*) that make a person do the same things repeatedly (*compulsions*). This could mean:

- Excessive handwashing.
- Putting things in a certain order and setting them up, often in a symmetrical way.
- Repeatedly checking locks or switches.
- Excessive cleaning of the space around you.
- Fear of seeking approval from others.

For me, growing up with a hoarder father was very difficult. Things were piled everywhere. I hated that I could never bring *people* over (I hesitate to say *friends* as I don't think I ever had any), then I would be extremely embarrassed by the few times people DID come over.

I didn't know this wasn't normal when I was young. My dad always needed things to be a certain way and in a certain spot. He would get very angry if things weren't in the right order, if you made a mistake, or if you didn't do things the way he liked.

When you add in a mother who was always anxious and worried about *everything*, things got even worse.

For example, she thought that it was dangerous to go out at night because we could be stabbed or robbed (even though we lived in a safe neighborhood, and this had never happened to anyone we knew).

As I grew older, this constant 'needing everything to be a certain way in a certain spot' (dad) and this constant 'disaster is at every turn' (mom), turned me into someone with OCD and GAD.

My OCD was more about doing rituals to satisfy my compulsions and keep bad things from happening. If I didn't do things according to my OCD, extreme anxiety would kick in. My mental issues would manifest in various ways, like picking at my nails, grinding my teeth, eating junk food ALL THE TIME, isolation, and so on.

Thankfully, today, I am better. And I owe this to a lot of hard work, self-reflection, support from a psychologist, prescribed medication, and focus on my physical and mental health.

My OCD and GAD are manageable, and I can live a pretty normal life. Again, Dialectic Behavior Therapy (DBT) has helped me a lot with this, and I'll discuss how in the next chapters.

Eating Disorders

Teens often have eating disorders, and teenage girls are likelier to have them than boys.[3] A person with an eating disorder has a bad relationship with food, body image, and exercise.

It happens to people of all ages, especially young adults who feel pressure to fit in. Teens are more likely to be obsessed with their weight because high school and the changes in their bodies at that age make them prone to this.

Eating disorders have many negative effects, such as:

- Dizziness and headaches.
- Hair loss and skin damage.
- Disturbed menstrual cycle.
- Unexplained and unhealthy weight loss and/or weight gain.

- Social anxiety.
- Fatigue and tiredness.
- Low self-esteem and lack of confidence.

Eating disorders are complicated and need to be treated in many different ways. Recovery is a long process that may take a long time and involve many different therapies and tools. DBT, as we will explore later, is a very strong technique to apply here.

Self-Harm

Technically, self-harm is not a mental health disorder. However, it is often a symptom of a serious mental issue, so it should never be taken lightly.

Statistics show that almost 17% of young adults indulge in self-harming behaviors.[4] Self-harm is when you hurt yourself to get rid of painful thoughts and feelings.

When life gets too hard, you may feel overwhelmed and helpless, which can make you experience sadness, numbness, loneliness, and hopelessness. These are very heavy, unhealthy emotions. And sometimes, it is better to physically feel pain (by committing self-harm) than to continue feeling these unpleasant emotions.

Self-harm can be caused by traumatic events like isolation, illness, assault, and family issues such as divorcing parents, sibling bullying, and so on.

Self-harm can include:

- Cutting and scratching yourself.
- Punching yourself.

- Pulling your hair.
- Burning your skin.
- Bruising yourself.

Depression

Depression affects 3% of 15- to 19-year-olds around the world. However, this statistic is way higher in the US, with about 13% of 12- to 17-year-olds experiencing a major depressive episode in 2020.[5] In the same year, 9% of young people in the US (approximately 2.2 million) were dealing with severe major depression.

Depression is a mental illness that makes people feel sad, think negatively, and lose motivation over and over again. Teens and young adults with depression often feel hopeless and alone, and they usually don't have the energy or motivation to do anything.

Examples of common signs of depression are:

- Changes in sleep or appetite.
- Inability to pay attention.
- Having less energy and drive.
- Not interested in activities or making friends.
- Hopelessness.
- Aches, pains, and general health problems.
- Thoughts of suicide.

Depression makes it very difficult for teens to go to school, get along with others, and do well in general. And no thanks to COVID-19, social withdrawal has made teens feel even more alone, which can make their depression worse.

I believe I was seriously headed into depression in my youth because of the severe loneliness I felt. I also experienced some of the symptoms above, just not all the time, but at different phases in my life. Another time I felt I was in depression was when I was attending graduate school in Hong Kong because I would study like a madman all night, and then sleep all day. (More on this on page 38.)

As I was not officially diagnosed with this, I cannot say for sure. But I know that had DBT not entered my life, I probably would've ended up clinically depressed as well.

What You Can Do to Move Forward

You can do many things to help your mental health if you are having trouble with any of the abovementioned mental health concerns. You can start by getting help from a supportive adult, like a teacher, a counselor, or your parents, or by working through this DBT workbook.

I would also suggest working with a therapist if you have access to one; this will help you get the most out of therapy.

However, if you don't, please know that this book is also designed for individuals who don't have access to individual therapy. The worksheets and exercises have been created to allow you to practice and develop DBT skills on your own. Now, let's move on to the first worksheet!

Worksheet: Game of Words

Let's see how many new terms you remember from Chapter 1.

The words from this chapter have been used to make this crossword puzzle.

Below, you'll find a description for each answer, which will help you fill in the blanks. Good luck!

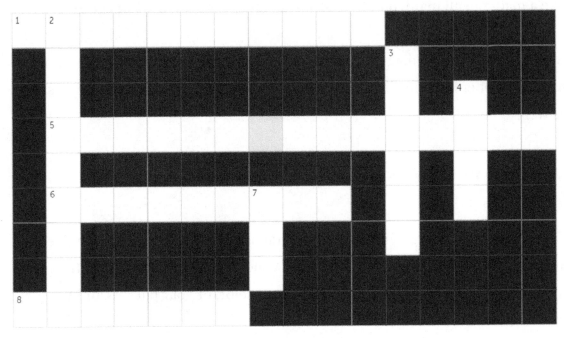

ACROSS

1 - Wanting to do the same things over and over again

5 - When you have a bad relationship with food, body image, and exercise

6 - To physically hurt yourself to get rid of painful thoughts and feelings

8 – Your body's natural 'warning sign'

DOWN

2 – Repeated, unwanted, and irrational thoughts

3 - Irrational, unrealistic fear

4 - Acronym for a neurodevelopmental disorder where it's hard to focus

7 Related to #6, minus the 'hyperactivity' factor

Chapter 2: DBT 101

"Acceptance doesn't mean resignation. It means understanding that something is what it is and there's got to be a way through it."
- Michael J. Fox

In this chapter, we'll look at DBT in more depth. We'll talk about what it is, how it works, and why it can help you with whatever you're going through right now.

What Is DBT?

Dialectic Behavior Therapy or **DBT** was created by Marsha M. Linehan[6] in the 1980s as a result of her and her colleagues' work with patients with borderline personality disorder (BPD). It is a type of Cognitive Behavioral Therapy (CBT).

But, while CBT focuses on finding negative thought patterns and changing them into positive ones (change-focused), Linehan thought it is much more effective to use two opposing (dialectical) tactics: Acceptance AND Change.

How Do Acceptance AND Change Work?

In other types of therapy, a lot of time is spent on the past. That is, you need to look and analyze your past or history to understand why you are where you right now.

In contrast, in DBT, you simply accept where you are right now. No need to deny it. No need to fight it. You accept what you're feeling and what you're going through. You accept your situation, and that's it. Linehan calls this **Radical Acceptance**.

The other half of DBT is **Change**. You've accepted your situation for what it is. Period. However, you know you don't want to keep feeling this way. And so you acknowledge that you need to make some changes to be happier at home, at school, in relationships, and in every other aspect of your life.

At first glance, it might sound weird to practice Acceptance and Change simultaneously. Still, if you think about it, it is possible to BE two different things at the same time.

For example, a person can be gentle and strong at the same time; someone can exhibit the characteristics of a team player and a leader at the same time.

Here's an example of practicing **Radical Acceptance** and **Change**. Say that you're experiencing *loneliness* in your life right now. You feel like you don't have any real friends and that there's no one to talk to about how you feel. The following is an example of how you can practice acceptance and change simultaneously.

ACCEPTANCE:

I'm feeling lonely right now.

I don't feel connected to anyone at the moment.

My parents don't understand me.

There are things I want to say, but I don't know how to say them or who to say them to.

It's okay not to be okay.

WHAT YOU CAN SAY TO YOURSELF:

"I accept myself for who I am right now. I'm lonely even though I don't know exactly why.

What I do know is that I'm not happy feeling lonely. So I accept myself now but I'm going to open myself to learning new things, meeting new people, and exploring myself to increase my happiness."

DESIRE TO CHANGE:

I am not as happy as I know I could be.

I AM OPEN TO

There's nothing wrong with wanting more.

I know that learning to be happy and not be lonely is going to be good for me.

I AM OPEN TO 'NEW'.

Radical Acceptance and Change are the foundations of DBT. It is from here that you will start to turn your life around.

Worksheet: Radical Acceptance and Change

Let's practice **Radical Acceptance** and **Change** right now, shall we?

1) Think of *anything* in your life that's not working for you or is not bringing you happiness.

2) Under **Acceptance**, write down statements that show your acknowledgment of the situation. (Important: Try not to provide any opinions (judgments) about the situation.)

3) Under **Desire to Change**, write down anything representing your desire to *move on* from the current situation. Write down any statement that suggests your willingness to change.

4) Under **What You Can Say to Yourself**, what would you like to say to yourself as you embrace Acceptance and Change? If you're having difficulty with this, imagine talking to a friend who's asking YOU for advice on the same situation. What would you say? Remember, BE KIND.

ACCEPTANCE: DESIRE TO CHANGE:

WHAT YOU CAN
SAY TO
YOURSELF:

NOTE: If you don't know what to write or are not ready to do the above exercise, that's okay. Take your time. Learn more about DBT below, and just go back to this worksheet when you feel ready.

How Does DBT Work?

Most of the time, DBT is used in these two main settings:

1. **Individual Therapy Sessions**: You are the main focus in this one-on-one setting. The therapist will form a therapeutic alliance with you to help you with your problems.

   They will pay special attention to self-destructive behaviors that could hurt you. These sessions focus on helping you learn and improve your social and coping skills to live a better life. Most of the time, these one-hour meetings happen once a week, especially in the first few months, to keep the process running smoothly and effectively.

2. **Group Therapy Sessions**: Similar to one-on-one sessions, these meetings focus on developing your skills. But instead of working one-on-one with a therapist, this method encourages you to work with a group of people while a trained therapist watches over the group. These meetings happen once a week and last for about two hours.

What Makes DBT Work?

The DBT framework is about improving your skills in the following four points.

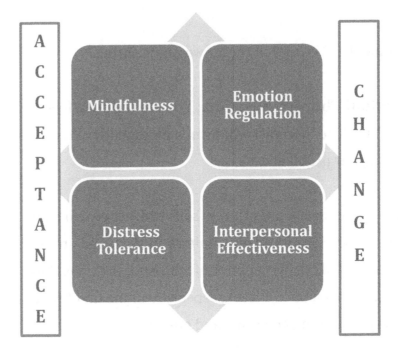

Let's take a quick look at each of these skills in more detail.

Mindfulness Skills

Mindfulness helps keep us in the present so that we're fully aware of what is happening in the here and now. It is split into two aspects – WHAT and HOW.

The *What* aspect deals with what you need to do to be more mindful, whereas the *How* skills focus on how you can bring mindfulness into your daily life.

WHAT Skills

These skills deal with **WHAT we need to do** to be more mindful.

- **Observe**: Start paying attention to what is happening inside and outside of you. Pay attention to how you feel and what's going on around you.

- **Describe**: Explain what you have seen in your own words. This step is done at the same time as observing.
- **Participate**: Be there in the moment to get the most out of it. You probably don't even notice it anymore, but you're doing A LOT of things simultaneously. For example, you're brushing your teeth (1) while reading texts on your phone, (2) thinking about breakfast, (3) thinking about your outfit for the day, (4) practicing in your head what to tell your teacher to escape gym class, etc. When was the last time you JUST brushed your teeth?!

HOW Skills

These skills focus on **HOW we can be more mindful** in our everyday lives.

- **Non-Judgmentally**: This skill teaches us to see things as they are and not jump to conclusions or judge them.
- **One-Mindfully**: This means to pay attention to one thing at a time and do it with awareness. This is also called getting in the flow.
- **Effectively**: Do what you think is right. As you develop, things that helped you in the past might not help you anymore. Learn to let these 'old systems' go and start doing what works for you now.

WHY YOU NEED THIS SKILL: You're being hit with so many things in your teenage life, and sometimes, it feels like they're all happening simultaneously. There are just too many things to process, which can lead to so much stress in your young life. Mindfulness will help you focus so that you can be more productive and efficient. It will also help you 'quiet' any chaos that you may be experiencing in your life.

IMPORTANT: To truly apply Mindfulness in your life, Mindfulness exercises (worksheets) are presented throughout the various mental health topics discussed in the following chapters.

Distress Tolerance or Reality Acceptance Skills

DBT distress tolerance skills teach you how to endure and handle upsetting situations in your life. Experiencing pain, being disappointed, and stressful events are all part of life. Denying them may work temporarily, but in the long run, it causes more harm.

Distress tolerance skills will teach you how to cope *while* stressful situations are happening. They also teach you the importance of learning from these events so that the next time something unpleasant happens, you will not be upset or hurt as much anymore.

WHY YOU NEED THIS SKILL: Teenage Years = High Stress.[7] You need this skill to endure and overcome these distressing situations and not act on unhealthy urges.

For example, say you accidentally tripped at school, and everyone around you started laughing. You feel very embarrassed and angry, and your 'urge' in this time of distress is to punch someone in the face. If you give in to this urge, you'll be in trouble (for deliberately physically hurting someone). If you don't give into this urge, you may be stewing in embarrassment for days.

But, with distress tolerance skills, you'll be able to 'tolerate' the situation (without giving in to your urge) and move on quicker from this event (instead of carrying it around you for a long time).

IMPORTANT: Like any important life skill, Distress Tolerance needs constant practice. Various exercises (worksheets) will be shown to you in the coming pages so that you can easily turn to them in your time of need.

Interpersonal Effectiveness Skills

DBT interpersonal effectiveness skills are about improving your interpersonal and intrapersonal communication skills, especially when you're upset or in conflict with someone. It's about how to keep your relationships healthy without losing yourself in the process.

As a Teen, you want to fit in. You want very much to belong and there's absolutely nothing wrong with that. That's perfectly normal. However, you may adjust too much to what others want in wanting to do this, losing yourself in the process.

With interpersonal effectiveness skills, you'll learn that balance between being agreeable to others while maintaining your self-respect.

WHY YOU NEED THIS SKILL: As a young adult, you'll find yourself in many NEW social relationships, which can be confusing and lead to mental health problems. You need this skill to know when to give way to what others want—and when not to.

IMPORTANT: Interpersonal Effectiveness exercises (worksheets) will be provided in the coming pages to help you learn this skill.

Emotion Regulation Skills

People say that young adults are just a ball of emotions. Well, that's OKAY. Again, this phase in your life is characterized by constant development and change, so experiencing roller coasters of emotions is part of that.

However, **your emotions are NOT who you are**. You can (and should) **feel your feelings; just don't act on them all the time**.

DBT emotion regulation skills help you do just that by teaching you how to:

- Recognize and describe your emotions.
- Identify roadblocks in changing and improving your emotional experiences.
- Focus on positive emotions while acknowledging any negative emotions.
- Bring mindfulness to existing emotions.

WHY YOU NEED THIS SKILL: When your behavior is based purely on your emotions, you'll probably regret most of your actions. This regret can bring guilt, make you feel sad, and may lead to depression. You don't want that, and you can prevent that with emotion regulation skills.

IMPORTANT: Emotion Regulation exercises (worksheets) are provided to you in this book under some of the mental health issues we'll be discussing in the next pages. Be sure to do these exercises to fully integrate these skills into your life.

Hopefully, you have a better understanding of DBT. Now, let's move on to the next chapters and discuss the common mental health challenges our teens are experiencing today and which DBT skills they can use to handle them.

Chapter 3: Anxiety, Stress, and Worry

"Go easy on yourself. Whatever you do today, let it be enough."
- Anonymous

Anxiety, stress, and worry are part of the human experience. Most of us have these kinds of feelings every day.

For teens, between managing school, family, activities, and friends, life can get pretty overwhelming. But I want you to know that there are ways to deal with your anxiety and stress to live a happy, well-balanced life as a teen.

Everyone responds to and deals with stress in their own way. A lot of it has to do with how our parents handled stressful situations themselves and how they taught us to handle our feelings. The blueprint you were given as a child continues throughout adulthood.

This is why we all respond differently to stressful situations. Some people see them as *challenges* to overcome. In contrast, others see them as *impossible obstacles* that they have no chance of defeating.

But here's the thing: whether you're great or terrible at dealing with stress or worry, there is always room for improvement. Humans are extremely adaptable!

We can unlearn old things holding us back and learn new ways of handling difficult situations better. It's never too late for change. By applying a few simple techniques in your daily life, you can become more effective in dealing with stress and worry.

Like most teens, school life takes up a large chunk of your life, and school is where you spend most of your time. However, if you suffer from anxiety, school can feel like running the gauntlet every day. This is an excerpt of one student's experience that may resonate with you:

I'm very lonely at school. I don't have a single friend there. Still, I make sure I arrive early because I dread being late. Just the thought of it makes me sweat bullets. I don't like being late because I know I won't be able to stand it when the other kids look up and stare at me if I ever enter the classroom late.

If you've ever felt like this, you're not alone. In fact, many people experience this more than you might think.

In this chapter, we will look at the differences between anxiety, stress, and worry. We'll also talk about what you can do to be more in control of your emotions and not freak out when something stressful happens.

Getting Personal: How Anxiety, Stress, and Worry Derailed My Life

When I was a young adult, my biggest worry was that I didn't know what to study in college or what I wanted to do with my life. In the Chinese culture, getting a good education is one of the most important things you can do. From a very young age, we are told that getting good grades will help us get into a good college, which will then help us get a well-paying job. If you don't achieve this, you'll be seen as a huge disappointment and bring great shame to your family. Talk about pressure.

As a child, I was into art and planned to become an animator. I studied art throughout high school, built up my portfolio, and applied to two of the best schools for animation in my city. When I didn't get into either program, I was in complete and utter panic!

I was in distress. I felt extreme pressure to get into ANY related program. I felt like if I didn't go to college right after high school, I would be a failure. I would be behind all my classmates who got into their programs.

After searching for art-related programs still accepting applications, I applied for multi-media design at another college outside my city. Fortunately, I got in. Whew!

However...

Even though it was a decent program and I made some friends, I quickly realized that multi-media design wasn't for me, so I dropped out after a semester. Later that year, I re-applied to another college in Ottawa and graduated with good grades two years later.

However...

Animation was not what I had imagined. I had no idea how much work was involved in creating a short movie. Even a short 10-second clip would take weeks of non-stop work. There were A LOT of all-nighters and deadlines. As you can imagine, this fueled my anxiety even more; soon enough, I felt burned out.

Although it was a great experience, I knew I did not want to work in the animation industry. I moved back home and reapplied to yet another university, where I would major in general arts before switching to sociology. I eventually graduated with a B.A. in Psychology. Since I'm the first person in my family to go to college, I'm very proud of this fact.

After I got my degree, I taught ESL (English as a Second Language) in Korea for a few years until I hit a plateau. To improve my career prospects, I attended a graduate school in Hong Kong to study for an M.A. in teaching English.

However...

I dropped out after only one semester. Even though I got great grades, I burnt myself out from study. I would often stay up all night doing research and sleep for most of the day. I wasn't making any friends in my program too. Soon enough, I lost all of my motivation and was starting to suffer from depression.

As you can see, **it had become a pattern in my life to start things but never finish them**. In total, I have studied in seven different programs and changed majors six times.

I realized later that **my mistake was using school to try and figure out what I wanted to do in life**. As a result, I wasted A LOT of time, energy, and money in the process.

What I should have done was take a step back, self-reflect, and spend some time figuring out what I wanted to do in life before committing to anything.

The craziest thing is that not a single company I worked for ever asked to see my grades or degree! It's only now I realize that I was worried and stressed out over nothing.

Don't get me wrong, education is important but 'getting good grades' is not the only thing in life. It is not your only measure of success. In fact, you will probably change jobs multiple times during your life.

A survey by the Bureau of Labor Statistics reveals that people between the ages of 18 and 24 change jobs an average of 5.7 times.[8] Also, you might not end up working in the field you thought you would. Many of my friends have jobs that have nothing to do with their college studies. As for me, I self-publish books and run an online business, which is a far cry from my animation and psychology days.

I'm sharing my story to illustrate the costs of letting anxiety, stress, and worry rule decisions in life.

In my mind, I must do 'A' to get to 'Z'. And if that didn't work, my knee-jerk reaction was to give up 'A' and try 'B' or 'C' or 'D' to get to 'Z'. It never occurred to me to take a moment and think if 'Z' is what I really wanted in life.

Also, say I realized that 'Z' is what I really wanted, I probably wouldn't have jumped from one thing to another if I had dealt with my anxiety, stress, and worry better. I could have just *stayed* with 'A'.

Now, before I show you the tools to better manage your worries, stress, and anxiety, let's take a closer look at each of them to gain a better understanding.

What is Worry?

Worry can be set off by too much negativity, feeling out of control, or thinking that life is giving you more than you can handle. Worries can sometimes be tough to control and make us behave in not-so-great ways.

Worry can sometimes be a great way to get you to deal with tough situations and problems that need to be solved. But if you constantly worry and can't stop thinking about bad things, this can become an anxiety disorder.

One of the best things you can do to avoid excessive worrying is to do a "Brain Dump". This is done by putting all your worries on paper or a notepad. This takes them out of your head and puts them into the physical world for you to see. Doing this allows you to view your worries clearly without having them take up your mental space.

You can start by ranking your worries in order of how bad you think they are and then seeing which ones are valid and need to be dealt with and which ones don't.

When you look at a worry, ask yourself if the thing that worries you is something you can control. If it is, think of something simple you can do to start dealing with it. But if you can't do anything about your worry (out of your control), it's best to forget it as best you can. Control (or the lack of it) is one of the main things that make us feel worried. If we feel like we're in charge, we worry less. When we don't feel like we're in charge of our lives, we tend to have more negative thoughts.

Example of a worry out of your control: Say you are worried about an earthquake happening in your city; is this something you can control? The answer is no unless you have this magic power to stop earthquakes.

Worrying about something you can't control is stressful and does you no good. So accept that you can't stop an earthquake from happening and stop thinking about the worst things that could happen if it does happen. Always worrying won't change the situation and will only stress you out.

Example of a worry you have control over: Say you are worried about failing a school exam. Is this something you can do something about? Yes!

So the next step is to figure out what you can do to pass the test, like spending more time studying. By studying, you can ensure that the thing that worries you (failing) won't happen.

For example, you can decide to study for two hours every night to get ready for the test. You can also ask your teacher questions about things you don't understand. You can also form a study group with a classmate or two to keep each other motivated. These are just some of the solutions you can adopt to increase your chances of passing the exam.

As you can see, this exercise shows you how to worry less and find real solutions. Sometimes, just writing down your worries can help you realize that your worries are not unbeatable or weren't that important after all.

Worksheet: Brain Dump

Step 1. Write down ONE THING you're worried about right now.

_____

_____

_____

_____

Step 2. Can you influence this worry in any way? Is this something under your control?

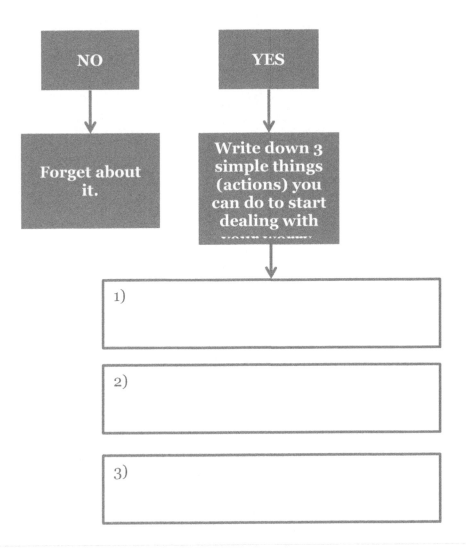

NO	YES

Forget about it.

Write down 3 simple things (actions) you can do to start dealing with

1)

2)

3)

What is Stress?

Compared to worry, which is cognitive and originates in the brain, stress has a more physiological manifestation. Stress is triggered by an external stressful event, and its symptoms can be felt in the body. It's our way of responding to external environmental changes or situations where we feel like we're being pushed beyond our limits. Stress can cause you to sweat a lot, make your heart beat faster, make it hard to breathe, and so on.

Just like worry, it can be good or bad. For example, suppose you have an assignment due the next day. In that case, the stress can (positively) push you to complete your assignment on time. You might feel the physical symptoms of stress for a short period, but once you hand in your assignment, the stress is released, and you feel fine again.

Chronic stress, however, is different. This is a state where you are stressed continuously for a long time. For example, say there's a bully in your class who always picks on you. This repeating stressor can cause chronic stress, leading to serious physical and mental health issues. So, it's important to know how to deal with stress in the short and long term.

What is Anxiety?

If worry is caused by negative thoughts and stress is manifested physiologically, anxiety is the culmination of both. Anxiety is your body's natural reaction to stress and worry, which it sees as a threat. It is made up of three parts.

Firstly, when your brain senses a threat or danger, it tells your body to go into a *fight-flight-freeze mode*. This kind of response helps you deal with things that might be dangerous. This can make you sweat, make your heart beat faster, make it hard to breathe, etc.

Secondly, there is the mental part, which includes *worrying thoughts* such as what will happen, what will I do, and why is this happening?

Lastly, there is an *emotional response* to worrying thoughts. This can include crying, screaming, anger, or shaking.

As you can see, when worry, stress, and anxiety are combined, this can take a huge toll on our mental and physical well-being. Just like worry and stress, anxiety is neither good nor bad. It keeps us safe and motivated and keeps us from being too complacent. However, too much stress for too long can cause anxiety disorders.

One of the most common mental health problems that teens face is anxiety disorders. In fact, according to data from the National Institute of Mental Health, 1 in 3 of all adolescents (13 to 18 years old) will likely experience an anxiety disorder.[9]

Now that you better understand worry, stress, and anxiety, let's look at how we can manage them more effectively.

DBT for Managing Stress, Worry, and Anxiety

Dialectical behavior therapy is based on the idea that everything is composed of opposites. Change happens when there is a dialogue between those opposing forces. So we cannot have just **Acceptance** or **Change**. It has to be **Acceptance** AND **Change**.

The goal of Acceptance AND Change is to help you arrive at your 'desired state'. In Acceptance, you acknowledge where you are NOW. However, something inside you tells you that you can be happier in life than in your current state. So this is where the Change part comes in. DBT aims to help you find and resolve this contradiction between your NOW and FUTURE self.

Mindfulness is the cornerstone of DBT, and it is very helpful in handling anxiety[10,11,12] because it teaches you how to improve your attention and focus. Mindfulness means *paying attention to the here and now* instead of thinking about the past or worrying about the future.

When you have time to yourself, simply sit with your thoughts and feelings for a while. Remember that your body needs to be still for your mind to be still. Sitting alone regularly in a quiet place can help you live your life with more awareness.

Remember too that 'being quiet' or meditation is not the only way to practice mindfulness. DBT also suggests the use of *grounding exercises* when dealing with anxiety. These exercises help you 'break' your thought process and bring you to the present, taking your focus away from your anxiety.

Here are some examples of grounding exercises:

1. Look for a specific-colored object in your room. Bring your whole focus on that object and describe it, e.g., *What is it? Where is it? What is its texture? What is its size? Is it light or heavy?*
   Examples: an orange, a flower, a ball, a pair of jeans, etc.

2. Sit outside and watch clouds pass by. Empty your mind of any other thoughts and just focus on the clouds. Find a shape you recognize, and see how slow or fast it moves. Watch it shape into something else.

3. During high stress, worry, or anxiety levels, put your hands on the part of your body where you feel most anxious. (For example, if you're nervous, you may want to put your hands over your stomach. If you're stressed and your heart is racing, you may want to put a hand over your heart.) Breathe in very slowly, and then breathe out even slower. Do this until you feel yourself calm down and relax.

Stress, worry, and anxiety take a huge toll on the mind and body. Left unchecked, they can become serious mental and physical health problems. Hopefully, this section has helped you differentiate between these three conditions and how DBT can help you address them.

However, as with many concepts, it is not just about understanding DBT. It's about putting it into practice.

So let's head on to some DBT exercises you can do to address any stress, worries, or anxieties you may have.

Worksheet: Grounding Technique Using Your 5 Senses

The purpose of grounding techniques is to connect you to the present so you can disconnect from your worries. Using your five senses—*sight, smell, sound, touch, and taste*—is an excellent way to ground yourself. Do this exercise anytime you feel stressed, worried, or anxious.

Remember, there is no right or wrong answer here. Don't evaluate or judge anything. Just provide what's being asked.

List 5 things you see right now. (e.g., umbrella, phone charger, laptop, water glass, clothes)

List 4 things you can touch right now. (e.g., book, desk, apple, pen)

List 3 things you can hear right now. (e.g., people, birds, piano music)

List 2 things you can smell right now. (e.g., orange peel, cologne)

List 1 thing you can taste right now. (e.g., gum)

Worksheet: Understanding How You Feel and Regulating Your Emotions

Sometimes, our emotions are hard to control because we don't fully understand them. This guide will help you describe your emotions. When you can properly define your feelings, it is easier to take control of them.

Step 1. Name the emotion.

I am feeling _____ right now.

Example: stressed, worried, scared, upset, etc.

Step 2. Identify what the emotion makes you want to do.

When I feel _____, it makes me want to

_____.

Example: When I feel <u>stressed</u>, it makes me want to <u>lock myself in my room and scream</u>.

Step 3. Identify the <u>cause</u> of your emotion.

What happened that triggered this emotion?

Example: I'm stressed because I have a quiz tomorrow.

_____

_____

Step 4. Describe your surroundings at the time of the event.

I am at/in:

_____

I notice:

_____

_____

Example: I am in <u>my bedroom</u>. I notice <u>my unmade bed, cluttered desk and the pile of books on it</u>.

Step 5. Identify your behavior and thoughts.

Example: When I felt <u>stressed</u>, I just <u>wanted to NOT deal with anything</u>. The thoughts that came to my mind are: <u>(1) what's the point of studying? I'll fail anyway, (2) Mom is really going to be mad if I fail another test, (3) I'll be grounded, so (4) I won't be able to attend my best friend's birthday this weekend</u>.

When I felt _____ (insert emotion),

I_____

_____

_____ (describe the behavior).

The thoughts that came to my mind are:

_____

_____

Step 6. Challenge the emotion.

Is feeling _____ appropriate? **Yes/No**

Does feeling _____ help my situation?**Yes/No**

Is this situation under my control?**Yes/No**

If **YES**, what can you do to <u>CHANGE the situation</u>?

Examples: stay home and study hard; ask mom for help on things I don't understand about this upcoming quiz, ask a classmate to come over so we can study together, etc.

_____

_____

_____

If **NO**, what can you do to <u>feel better</u>?

Examples: do mindfulness exercises, watch funny videos, take a nice and long shower, etc.

_____

_____

_____

Chapter 4: ADHD / ADD

"Whatever you do, don't look at it (ADHD) as a disability, and hopefully, whatever is helping you understand it will show you the great things about how you can use it to your benefit and not just feel like you have some curse upon you."

- *Channing Tatum*

A few years ago, I had coffee with an old friend. She was working as a high school research project mentor during that time, and I could see the worry and exhaustion in her entire demeanor. When I asked her how things were going, she said she was having trouble with one of her students:

"I have a student that has so much potential. I don't understand what is going on with him. He would always come up with the best ideas. Then his focus would shift. I met with him yesterday, and our talk about his research project went well. After the meeting, he was supposed to send me an email with his progress report, but I never got one.

I followed up with him in the morning. He admitted he didn't remember the task; this had happened several times before. I spoke to other teachers regarding this issue I was facing with him. They shared that he has been sleeping in class. When he is awake, he has trouble paying attention. His thoughts keep jumping from one thing to another. At this point, I don't know what to do or how to help him."

When I heard her story, my mind began to connect the dots. I shared my thoughts with her—the student was possibly struggling with ADHD. A few weeks later, when I saw my friend again, I asked about her student. She said she talked to his parents and that they had consulted a doctor to figure out what was going on. The child was diagnosed with ADHD and is now getting the right help to improve his focus.

In this chapter, we'll talk in-depth about ADD and ADHD, including how it affects your life at home, school, and other places. We will also talk about how DBT can help you deal with this.

What is ADHD?

ADHD is a common neurodevelopmental disorder usually found in children but can last into adulthood. It is a mental health issue that can make it hard for kids to do the things they need daily. Things like making plans for the day or taking part in conversations can be scary and hard for people with ADHD.

ADD vs. ADHD

ADD is AD<u>HD</u>, minus the Hyperactive component. In 1994, the medical community decided the official name of the condition to be ADHD because it covered both inattentive and hyperactive forms of the disorder.

<u>ADHD Symptoms</u>

When someone hears 'ADHD' the immediate image in their minds is someone who's *hyperactive* and *unfocused*. But what does that look like, really? Following is a more detailed list of ADHD symptoms.

1. **Predominantly <u>Inattentive</u> Presentation of ADHD**

Young adults who have this condition are not hyperactive at all. People say that children with this type of ADHD are shy or lost in their worlds, and their energy levels aren't that high. The danger with this form of ADHD is that symptoms are not always noticed because people who have them are often thought to be daydreamers or people who like putting things off.

Its symptoms include:

- Easily getting off track and distracted
- Difficulty paying attention
- Difficulty coping with long tasks (e.g., school assignments)
- Difficulty staying focused on the task at hand
- Being disorganized
- Being forgetful
- Struggling with active listening during conversations
- Difficulty paying attention to details
- Easily misplacing items (e.g., pens, notebooks, clothing items, etc.)
- Making seemingly careless mistakes
- Having trouble understanding, making sense of, and carrying out instructions

2. **Predominantly <u>Hyperactive-Impulsive</u> Presentation of ADHD**
   Kids dealing with the predominantly hyperactive-impulsive presentation of ADHD have high energy levels. You will see these kids jumping around, and it can be hard for them to sit still. Definitely, this kind of ADHD stands out more.

Its symptoms include:

- Fidgeting and tapping
- Running around unnecessarily

- Performing high movement activities at seemingly inappropriate times (.e.g., leaving your side and climbing a tree all of a sudden)
- Difficulty staying quiet
- Constantly interrupting others
- Talking frantically
- Talking too fast and cutting people off (e.g., answering a question before the teacher even has a chance to finish it)
- Impatience
- Chatting excessively
- Impulsiveness
- Not able to stay in one place for a long time (e.g., getting up and moving around in the middle of dinner.)
- Always being "on the go"

3. **Combined Presentation of ADHD (Inattentive + Hyperactive)**

In the combined presentation, a child has symptoms of both inattentive and hyperactive types of ADHD.

Remember that having any or some of these symptoms doesn't necessarily mean you have ADHD. If you are worried that you might have ADHD, reach out and talk to a supportive adult such as your parents, favorite teacher, counselor, etc.

DBT for ADHD

DBT helps you look at your thoughts, feelings, and life in a more balanced way. It tries to get you to stop seeing things in black and white and start seeing them in shades of gray.

This is especially important when addressing ADHD. For example, as mentioned above, one of inattentive ADHD's symptoms is *low energy*. A person having this challenge would then need techniques that promote *high energy* to balance their way of living.

Acceptance and validation are important parts of DBT. It's about recognizing and accepting difficult emotions that emerge from challenging situations. It teaches you to accept your pain instead of trying to hide it. Linehan, the creator of DBT, believes that when you deny or push down difficult emotions, they will return to the surface later. In contrast, if you let yourself feel and think about the things that make you uncomfortable, it makes you more likely to act and solve your problems.

In DBT, the dialectical way of thinking (i.e., viewing a situation from multiple, often opposite perspectives) helps us get past the idea that there is only one right way to do things. Everyone is different, so why apply a 'one size fits all' mentality?

I remember a friend telling me about an adolescent client with a predominantly inattentive form of ADHD. As a result, the client couldn't focus on studying and failed his classes. So instead of using a template, the young adult was given a personalized study plan: study for 30 minutes and then take a 10-minute break. He had to do these three more times. After that, he can take a longer break. This method helped the client stay focused and get more school work done!

Mindfulness and Interpersonal Effectiveness

In this section, we'll look at how **Mindfulness** and **Interpersonal Effectiveness**, two DBT core skills, can be used to deal with ADHD.

In today's interconnected world, it seems like something always needs to be done. Even though this may seem helpful sometimes, it keeps us from living in the moment. And with countless distractions and device notifications throughout the day, it can be extremely difficult for anyone with ADHD to focus on one thing at a time.

Mindfulness

Mindfulness helps because it teaches us how to be in the here and now. It reminds us to live in the present rather than bounce back and forth between the past and the future. It also enhances our ability to control our attention and helps us regain and sustain focus when it starts to wander.

In particular, mindfulness meditation can be helpful when addressing ADHD.[13] It thickens our prefrontal cortex, the part of the brain that helps us focus, plan, and keep our impulses in check. It also speeds up the release of dopamine (also known as the "feel-good hormone") in the brain, which is low in people with ADHD.

Interpersonal Effectiveness

People with ADHD often act in ways that aren't helpful or healthy. This can make it hard for them to get along with other people and form healthy relationships.

Interpersonal effectiveness is the DBT technique that will help you create and keep good relationships with yourself and others.

The following are some of the benefits of interpersonal effectiveness:

- It helps you understand your needs in a relationship.
- It helps you effectively consider others' needs in a relationship.
- It helps you become more aware of the way you talk and listen.
- It teaches you to be more assertive so that your needs and wants will be heard when you talk about them.
- It helps you learn how to 'stand up for yourself'.

- It helps you set clear boundaries and how to let people know when they cross them.
- It helps you learn how to deal with relationship conflicts before they become serious problems.

Worksheet: Soap Bubble Breathing

Soap Bubble Breathing is a mindful breathing exercise that will help you be in the moment.

1. Breathe in deeply.
2. Hold your breath for a moment.
3. As you breathe out, imagine slowly blowing out a soap bubble.
4. Remember not to blow too hard. You don't want the imaginary soap bubbles to pop.
5. Imagine the soap bubbles forming and taking flight. Follow their path in your mind.
6. Repeat steps 1-4 until you feel more centered.

A Note to Parents and Teachers on How to Help Children with ADHD

Because ADHD can appear early on, parents and teachers of kids with ADHD should work closely together.

For parents, I understand that having a child with ADHD can be challenging. Please remember that praising them and focusing on their strengths is often more effective than focusing on their ADHD-related traits.

Also, it's important to involve your teen in taking care of their condition instead of just telling them what to do. For example, if you want to limit how much time they spend in front of a screen, talk to them and agree on a timeframe when they can use their gadgets.

Involving teens in the process makes them less likely to feel controlled. Instead, this method will teach them to be responsible, making them feel respected and empowered.

At this stage, it is very helpful for parents and teachers to talk to each other. It's important for teens with ADHD to have a smooth transition between home and school because that keeps their surroundings consistent. Setting routines in these two most important parts of their lives gives them stability.

For example, when a parent communicates to the school that their child has ADHD, teachers can help by using alternative learning methods. And then, they can observe the behavior of such students and provide constructive feedback to parents. This feedback helps in the child's overall well-being and treatment.

Parents and teachers can carve out an action and recovery plan as well. These rules can help hold children with ADHD accountable when they indulge in unacceptable behaviors.

For instance, depending on the severity of their aggressive behavior, parents can take away certain privileges, such as their PlayStation, for a few days. At school, teachers can give detention to hold them accountable. Consequences like these will provide the space and time for young adults with ADHD to reflect on their actions. However, parents and teachers should explain why they are doing this and that it is for their good.

Many young adults with ADHD have trouble reading social cues and making friends. Parents and teachers can make a huge difference in this area by seeking out activities and social groups that share the same interests as their children. Such activities and groups can boost their confidence and social skills and help them build friendships.

Scouting is a great example for teens with ADHD to thrive. Camping, climbing, and other group activities help them meet their need for physical activity and burn any extra energy they have. Remember that Scout leaders need to know about your teen's condition to guide and check up on them properly.

Worksheet: DEARMAN

This DBT exercise will help you learn how to ask for something respectfully and effectively, which will help you build and keep relationships no matter how your request turns out.

For example, say you're extremely annoyed because your sibling is taking your clothes without asking for permission. Without meaning to, your ADHD may cause you to blurt out your frustration in a very brutal and scathing way that may harm your relationship with your sibling.

DEARMAN helps you get your messages across without damaging your relationships. It helps you be more assertive while keeping the other person's feelings in mind.

Fill out your response against each acronym in the spaces provided below.

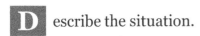 **D** escribe the situation.

When you are describing an incident or situation, do so clearly. Avoid mentioning your opinions and stick to the facts.

Example: You took my favorite shirt out of the closet and used it today.

Your turn:

_____

_____

E xpress how you are feeling about the situation.

Use 'I' statements to keep the communication open when sharing your emotions. When you make assumptions and use 'you' statements, this increases the chances of a conflict.

Example: I feel frustrated when you take my clothes without permission.

Your turn:

_____

_____

A ssert yourself.

Say what you want to happen clearly but not aggressively. This will help the other person understand you better.

Example: Please ask me first before you wear my clothes.

Your turn:

_____

_____

R eninforce your request.

Let the other person know that your request is important. So say how much you will appreciate it if you get what you want or need.

Example: I would appreciate it if you did that. I would feel so much better and not get frustrated about where my clothes were.

Your turn:

_____

_____

M indfulness.

Remain mindful of your words and emotions; stay focused and remain on topic. As someone with ADHD, this may be hard for you, so it might be a good idea to practice what you're going to say in front of the mirror first.

Example: So, I hope you understand why I'm requesting this. (Note: Aside from your words, ensure your body language is also mindful. For example, don't raise your voice and maintain a relaxed composure.)

Your turn:

_____

_____

A ppear confident.

Show confidence through your words and body language. Do not apologize.

Example: Sit or stand up straight, straighten your shoulders, maintain eye contact, and then say: I hope I'm getting across to you because my feelings won't change. I'll always want anyone who wants to wear my clothes to ask permission first.

Your turn:

_____

_____

N egotiate.

Negotiate if the person you're talking to doesn't want to grant your request. This will allow you both to find an acceptable solution to a problem. Keep an open mind and listen to the other person's point of view too.

Example: How about we just try it? Next time you want to wear any of my clothes, just ask. If you do that, I'll remember to always knock on your bedroom door before going in.

Your turn:

_____

_____

Worksheet: GIVE

People with ADHD find it difficult to connect with others, so it's important that others know and feel that you're also considering *their* wants and needs. You do this by showing **I**nterest when they talk and when you **V**alidate (acknowledge) what they say to you.

Also, people often say no to a request not because they don't want to give what you want but because of *how* you ask for it. So it's important to appear **G**entle and display an **E**asy Manner when communicating a request.

G	I	V	E
Gentle	**Interested**	**Validate**	**Easy Manner**
Be gentle. Avoid insulting the other person. Be nice and respectful so that the other person doesn't feel attacked.	**Show your interest** in the other person by actively listening to them.	**Acknowledge** the other person's feelings and emotions. Don't be judgmental and show that you truly understand them.	Adopt a **friendly and easy-going** manner. A warm and inviting personality makes others feel comfortable and more accepting of your requests.
What do you want to DO?			
List 3 ways you can ask for something in a *gentle* way. *(e.g., use a friendly and soft tone when speaking)*	List 3 ways you can show that you are *interested* in a conversation. *(e.g., make eye contact)*	List 3 ways you can offer *validation* to others. *(e.g., say 'hmmm' or nod when agreeing with what the other person says)*	List 3 ways to show that you are *easy to get along with*. *(e.g., smiling, not folding your arms across your chest when talking)*

G	I	V	E
1.	1.	1.	1.
2.	2.	2.	2.
3.	3.	3.	3.

What do you want to SAY?			
Example: I don't mean to make you feel bad, but I am not happy in this situation.	*Example: You look worried; what are you thinking?*	*Example: I hear you. Let me think about this some more.*	*Example: Hey, look at us, sulking like kids. Why don't we take a breather and discuss this more later?*

Chapter 5: Phobias

"Being brave isn't the absence of fear.
Being brave is having that fear but finding a way through it."
- Bear Grylls

Getting Personal: I'm Afraid of Blood

I have an intense fear of blood (*hemophobia*). Sometimes it is so bad that it sends shivers down my spine whenever I see it. It makes up a part of my anxiety and OCD. Oddly though, this phobia doesn't surface when I watch action movies that can be quite violent and bloody.

Once in a public washroom, I totally freaked out after noticing what I believed was a blood stain on the toilet seat. I thought I might have contracted some disease because I may have touched the blood. At that moment, I pulled out my phone and started googling my chances of getting a disease, even though I knew that was not how contamination works. For infection, the blood would have to be fresh and contain germs. It then had to come into contact with a cut or open wound on my body. So, the chances of getting infected with a disease by sitting on a toilet seat were close to zero.

However, in my agitated state, there was no way for my logical brain to understand that. So there I was, trembling in fear despite my brain telling me there's nothing to fear.

What are Phobias?

A phobia is an uncontrollable and illogical response to something out of fear or worry. It is known to be stronger than a simple fear. Unlike general anxiety-based disorders, something specific triggers phobias. When facing the origin of this fear, you may undergo an unfathomable sense of panic or dread. The source can be anything from an object, place, location, or environment.

A phobia can be anything from mild irritation to serious problems that make your life hard. Even if you know that the fear is often irrational, it can make you feel helpless.

About 19 million Americans have at least one mild to severe phobia.[14] You should see a doctor if your phobia is getting in the way of your overall quality of life. If you don't get help from an expert and let the fear go on for too long, it can take over your life. Fortunately, thanks to DBT, my fear of blood is much better now, so I don't freak out when I see it or have to use a public bathroom.

Phobia Symptoms

Symptoms of phobias can occur whenever you face the object of your phobia. Sometimes, just the thought of the feared object, place, location, or environment can trigger the phobia. This is known as *anticipatory anxiety*.

Symptoms can include the following:

- Nauseousness
- Dizziness
- Perspiration and sweating
- Rapid palpitations or increased heartbeats
- Trembling
- Difficulty breathing or shortness of breath
- Fear that you may be dying
- Losing a sense of reality

- Having an upset stomach
- Obsessing about the source of the anxiety

Phobias are an interesting phenomenon. Phobias may not affect your daily life unless you frequently encounter what you fear. However, the road to normalcy can be difficult for people with a complex phobia.

Agoraphobia is an example of a complex phobia. In this anxiety disorder, a person is terrified of being trapped in a situation or environment from which they believe escape will be difficult if something goes wrong. They are afraid to be trapped with no chance of help coming their way.

The most significant disadvantage of having this phobia is that it restricts your daily routine. For example, you might avoid entering an elevator because you're afraid of becoming stuck without assistance, resulting in a panic attack. To avoid this, you take the stairs to your office, even though it is on the 12th floor. Although you may not be afraid of being in confined spaces (*claustrophobia*), agoraphobia can cause you to avoid certain situations entirely.

If someone finds themselves in this situation, they may experience increased fear and, eventually, a full-fledged panic attack. As a result of trying to avoid these attacks, the individual may develop a social anxiety disorder (SAD). This condition was previously known as *social phobia*.

People who suffer from SAD avoid social gatherings and prefer solitude because the fear of something bad happening surpasses any desire to connect with others. As you can imagine, this isolation makes it difficult to maintain relationships and navigate daily life.

Types of Phobias

The American Psychiatric Association categorizes phobias into three types:

1. **Agoraphobia.** As previously stated, this phobia is the fear of becoming trapped in a situation or location where no help is available. In some extreme cases, this anxiety can be so intense that the person becomes afraid to leave their home.

2. **Specific phobias.** These phobias are associated with a specific object or item, such as spiders, snakes, and so on. There are four types of specific phobias.

   - Environmental: fear of tornadoes, water, mudslides, lightning, etc.
   - Situational: fear of leaving home, crossing bridges, driving, etc.
   - Medical: fear of doctors, needles, or blood.
   - Animals: fear of spiders, birds, snakes, cats, etc.

3. **Social phobias**. This is a severe fear of being in a social gathering or setting. Social phobias can revolve around a specific social situation (e.g., public speaking) or generalized, where someone fears doing something in the presence of others because they're worried about being judged or humiliated (e.g., giving a presentation).

Now that we've discussed the various types of phobias, let's look at some of the DBT tools available to help cope with this mental condition.

DBT for Phobias

> *"When you explore your fears, then you set yourself free."*
> — *Stephen Richards*

Mindfulness

It is exhausting to be constantly in fear about something. It stresses you and impairs your ability to recognize and respond to challenges because you're never just in the moment.

We're often so busy contemplating the past or worrying about the future that we forget to live in the present. We lose our sense of reality and frequently perceive it incorrectly. This is called *cognitive distortion*, and it causes anxiety because we are either thinking about what we did wrong (past) or what we might do wrong (future). This is a lose-lose situation because there's nothing you can do to change the past, and you can't control the future.

Mindfulness is one of the most effective tools for dealing with this because it's all about being fully aware of the present moment. You are not in the past or the future. You are just here.

By completely immersing yourself in the present, you will be better able to deal with future challenges as they arise. Being more mindful reduces anxiety by cultivating a positive attitude and remaining grounded during stressful situations.

A study published in the *Journal of Cognitive Psychotherapy* on mindfulness and task concentration in people suffering from social phobias found promising results. The participants found the treatment "well accepted and highly effective" after nine 45- to 60-minute mindfulness and task concentrating sessions.[15]

Worksheet: Box Breathing

1. Close your eyes and breathe in for a count of four.
2. Hold that breath for a count of four.
3. Release your breath for a count of four.
4. Stay still for another count of four.
5. Repeat steps 1-4 for three (3) minutes.

Self-Soothe

"Sometimes just a little bit of light is enough
to turn phobias into fluttering butterflies."

— Marina Matiss

As the quote implies, a distraction is sometimes all that's required to break the cycle of worry and panic and return to a more relaxed state of mind.

Self-soothing exercises help you stay calm by diverting your attention to physical stimuli. I do this several times a day to bring myself back to the present moment so I don't give in to my fears.

Worksheet: Self-Soothe with ONE Sense

As previously mentioned, your body perceives physical stimuli through the five senses: *touch, smell, taste, see, and hear.* (See Grounding Technique Using Your 5 Senses on page 46).

In the exercise below, though, we'll focus on one sense. Choose the ONE stimulus that is most soothing to you, and then on the space provided, write down what you want to do for at least five (5) minutes.

☐ **Touch**: _____

    Example: glide my hand over my pet's soft fur

☐ **Smell**: _____

    Example: smell my favorite scent

☐ **Taste**: _____

    Example: drink calming green tea

☐ **See**: _____

    Example: cute baby videos on YouTube

☐ **Hear**: _____

    Example: listen to my favorite song

Distress Tolerance

"When you have fear then the world is a big place.
When you have courage then the world shrinks."
— Stephen Richards

Distress Tolerance, or the ability to manage actual or perceived emotional distress, is one of the most difficult DBT skills to master.

How we perceive our ability to face and tolerate distress defines how we avoid our phobias. They are indirectly proportional to one another. If our distress tolerance level is high, we're better at dealing with our phobias and vice versa.

Example: Angie has acrophobia (fear of heights) and a low distress tolerance level. So she will most likely never go to the rooftop of a building. In fact, just the thought of it can make her sweat bullets. A colleague, Gary, has acrophobia, too, but his distress tolerance level is high. So Gary will never volunteer to go to the rooftop, but he can tolerate it if he has to.

Mindfulness and Radical Acceptance are two distress tolerance skills that people with phobias can use to reduce their negative emotional responses when faced with their fears.

"Mindfulness training increased distress tolerance on the hyperventilation challenge", according to a 2019 study on the effect of short mindfulness training (15 mins) on distress tolerance and stress reactivity. In addition, *"Mindfulness training led to reduced urges to neutralize an upsetting thought."*[16]

Radical Acceptance is when you completely accept a stressful situation—without judgment.

If people with phobias can learn this DBT skill, it can change their lives. Instead of figuring out why they have phobias, radical acceptance asks you to face the stressful situation and detach yourself from it. You don't need to 'dig deeper'; you just have to accept the situation to move on.

We think that if we fully understand a situation, it will turn out differently. But that's not always the case. In truth, when we 'dig deeper', we often feel worse, not better. We're prolonging our suffering (of the situation).

Besides, always *thinking* about something won't change anything; *acting* on them does. So, letting yourself get caught up in negative thoughts (e.g., Why do I have this phobia? Why am I like this? etc.) will just hurt your emotional health and make you think that things will never get better.

How to Cope with Phobia(s)

Fear is part of being human. Phobias, however, are on another level because it makes people change their lives to stay away from what they fear. Here are some ways to deal with your irrational and out-of-control reactions to whatever you fear.

1. MIND your feelings. (THINK about how you feel.)

First, you need to be aware of and accept your feelings. Once you become aware of and acknowledge the fear, you can control how you approach it. Give that emotion a name and address it. For example, say '*I feel very irritated, so I will remove myself from this setting. I'm better off spending some time alone than getting so distressed.*'

Use your courage to remind yourself that this emotion is NOT you. It doesn't control you. Yes, it is okay to feel afraid but realize that fear is just an emotion—nothing more, nothing less. Once you feel anxious or scared, please don't dwell on it for too long. Acknowledge the fear, accept it, and release the feeling. (Radical acceptance!)

2. Prove your fears wrong.

Take a step back when you feel like your fears are taking over. Close your eyes and picture yourself as a lawyer making a case against your fears.

You can either write down your worries or talk about them one by one. For example, you might be afraid to give a presentation in class because you might forget some of the points you want to make. To deal with this and show yourself that you have nothing to worry about, tell yourself, *'Everything will be fine!'* because you have practiced your speech so much that you know it by heart.

The goal is to come up with as many reasonable and logical reasons as possible to feel better. Once you've written down your reasons, you'll find that your fear isn't as big and scary as it seems.

Worksheet: Validating Fears

1. Write down each of your fears.
2. Ask yourself if the fear is valid.
3. Debunk each fear by making a case against it.
4. If you are unable to debunk a specific fear, write down what actions you can take to address it.

Specific Fear	Is the fear valid? (Yes/No/Not sure)	If yes, why is this fear valid? List your reasons.	If not, why is this fear invalid? List your reasons.	Action(s) you can take to address the fear.
Example:				
I'm worried I will forget something and screw my school presentation.	Not sure.	Other students might laugh at me.	I've been practicing my presentation for a whole week already.	Continue to practice. Think positively. Realize that no one is perfect.
Your turn:				

3. Gradually confront your fears.

To confront your fears, you can use a DBT skill called **Opposite Action**. This skill requires you to act differently despite every fiber of your being telling you to act another way.

For example, when confronted with your phobia, you feel very scared, and your natural response might be to escape by running away from the situation. So, in the example we have above, you might want to call in sick to avoid giving your school presentation.

Instead, it would help if you moved toward the thing that's making you afraid. So, to continue with our last example, DON'T call in sick. And when it's your turn to present, take a deep breath, slowly get up from your desk, and walk towards the front of the class. Face your classmates, make eye contact, and give them a warm smile, even though you're freaking out inside. Start your presentation when you're ready. Do the exact opposite of what your fear tells you to do.

Doing things that make you face your fears will help you get your sense of control back over time. Start small with less scary things and work your way up to scarier things. For example, start by presenting in front of the mirror, then to your family, then to your friends, and finally in front of the class.

Even people believed to be the bravest feel fear. The important thing is to deal with it instead of letting it control you. When you are scared, don't let it restrict you or stop you from fulfilling your objective or goal. Remember that fear is just like any emotion, and once you learn how to manage it, you will realize that you can do anything to which you put your mind. There is no end to what you can achieve.

Worksheet: Rating Your Fear

In the table below, write down your fears and rate each on a scale from 1-10, with 1 meaning the fear is not scary and 10 means it causes extreme panic. Next, write down one action you can take to address the fear and reduce its impact. Finally, list down some ways that will help you increase your chances of facing your fear instead of avoiding it. (This last step helps to hold you accountable.)

Fear	Fear Rating 1 = Not Scary 10 = Extreme Panic	Action(s) I Can Take to Minimize Fear's Impact	Ways to Force Myself to Face My Fear
Example:			
Being stuck in an elevator.	*8*	*1-Take the escalator often so I get used to the 'moving' feeling.* *2-Slowly get used to being alone in a confined space. I can stay in my bedroom alone for 30 mins. Then I can go to the basement alone for 15 mins, and so on.*	*Tell my mom about this and say I'll do house chores if I don't stick to my plan.*

Fear	Fear Rating 1 = Not Scary 10 = Extreme Panic	Action(s) I Can Take to Minimize Fear's Impact	Ways to Force Myself to Face My Fear

Worksheet: ACCEPTS

This DBT Distress Tolerance exercise is called **ACCEPTS**. It will help you distract yourself while in the middle of a stressful situation, which in turn will help your emotions subside.

To complete this worksheet, think of a phobia from which you suffer and imagine coming face to face with it.

A ctivities.

List actions you find stimulating and require your focus.

Examples: drawing, singing, yoga, etc.,

Your turn:

_____

_____

C ontributing.

Shift your focus to someone else. Doing good for others will help you feel good and distract you from your turmoil.

Examples: donate old clothes, volunteer to cut the grass for someone

Your turn:

_____

_____

C omparisons.

Think of a previous situation that is worse than the fear you have now.

Example: I fell off my bike and broke my arm, and it was very painful. I had to be in a cast for a whole month.

Your turn:

_____

_____

E motions.

Counter your fears by doing something opposite to how you feel. When you do something different, your emotions will alter.

Example: Feeling panicky? Do some mindful breathing exercises.

Your turn:

_____

_____

P ush away.

Instead of giving in to your fears, push them away (as opposed to denying that they're there). Choose what you want to do from the list below. Feel free to add more options too.

☐ Go into an empty room and say, in a loud voice, **STOP! GO AWAY!**

☐ Write down your fears and negative thoughts on a piece of paper and then let them go by burning the paper.

☐ Go for a walk. Pick up a stone. Imagine that the stone represents your fears, and then throw the stone as hard as you can.

☐ Write down your fears and negative thoughts on a piece of paper, crumple the paper into a ball, and throw it into a trash can.

☐ Others:

_____

_____

T houghts.

Think happy thoughts to bring yourself to a happy place and time.

Examples: Look at pictures of a previous vacation or birthday party; watch a feel-good movie; sing a song that brings happy memories.

Your turn:

_____

_____

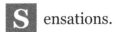 ensations.

Bring yourself to the present by using the <u>Grounding exercise</u> on page 46.

Worksheet: IMPROVE

This DBT Distress Tolerance exercise is called **IMPROVE**. This skill encourages you to make a conscious effort to *improve* the moment.

Think of a time when you were suffering from your phobia, and then use the prompts below to understand how you can improve such a situation.

I	Imagery. Imagine positive scenarios.	Imagine yourself handling your phobia extremely well and how amazing you feel afterward. Visualize that moment in your head. What did you imagine? Example: I imagine myself smiling and feeling very proud of myself. I then go and treat myself to a coffee date with friends. Your turn: _____ _____ _____
M	Meaning. Find meaning in your stressful situation. What good came out of it?	What meaning did you find in your stressful situation? Example: The distress made me realize I'm stronger than I thought I was. Your turn: _____ _____ _____

P	Prayer.	Turn to a higher being for strength and comfort. (Note: If you're not religious, turn to someone you admire and seek their guidance.)
		Example: Go to church, sit on one of the pews and ask for strength.
		Your turn:
		_____
		_____
		_____
R	Relaxation.	Engage in relaxing activities to calm yourself and clear your mind. List down three activities you find relaxing.
		Example: reading a book, painting, taking long walks
		1 _____
		2 _____
		3 _____
O	One thing at a time.	Put your mind in the present moment. Don't think of anything apart from the ONE THING you're doing right now.
		Example: I'm drinking calming tea. I'm deeply inhaling its aroma. I take a slow sip and let the flavor stay on my tongue as long as I can. I put my

		mug down and savor the tea's soothing effect on me.
		What are you doing? _____ _____ Describe this moment. _____ _____ _____
V	**Vacation.**	Disengage and take a mental break. Example: take a long warm bath, play a video game for 30 mins, get in bed and take a nap, etc. Your turn: _____ _____ _____
6 **E**	**Encouragement.**	Boost yourself up. Say positive affirmations to yourself. Example: I am enough. I am a good person. I am stronger than my fears. Today is a good day to have a great day. I am grateful for what I have. Write down five (5) positive affirmations you can use for yourself. 1 _____

2

3

4

5

Chapter 6: PTSD & Panic Disorders

"There is no timestamp on trauma. There isn't a formula that you can insert yourself into to get from horror to healed. Be patient. Take up space. Let your journey be the balm."

— Dawn Serra

Understanding PTSD

Post-traumatic stress disorder (PTSD) used to be called battle fatigue syndrome or shell shock. It is a long-term condition that develops after a very stressful event. People can get PTSD after being in or going through things that make them feel afraid, helpless, hurt, threatened, or horrified. PTSD is a serious condition that affects a sufferer's daily life.

Some things that can cause PTSD are being sexually or physically assaulted, losing a loved one suddenly, being in an accident, a terrorist attack, war, or a natural disaster. PTSD can also affect the families of these victims and the people who helped save them.

People react differently when they go through traumatic events, and they can demonstrate anxiety, fear, anger, surprise, guilt, or shame. Some people can have these reactions for a long time (more than a month), and it can get so bad that it's hard to function normally.

According to the National Center for PTSD, 15-43% of girls and 14-43% of boys go through at least one traumatic event. From this experience, 3-15% of girls and 1-6% of boys develop PTSD.[17]

PTSD Causes

People react differently to traumatic events that they've experienced. So even if two people are exposed to the same traumatic event, it doesn't mean both will develop PTSD.

Also, our support systems are a big part of how PTSD affects us and how we deal with it. We are less likely to get PTSD if we have a caring family, helpful friends, and qualified professionals around us.

For young adults, PTSD is more likely to happen when exposed to abuse (mental, emotional, physical, or sexual) or if they are in a very stressful environment (at home or school).

Adolescents who have a higher risk of developing PTSD include:

- Those who suffer from other mental health issues.
- Have mental health conditions that run in the family.
- Have alcohol or drug problems.
- Are often the victims of bullying.

Common traumatic events that can cause PTSD include the following:

- Natural disasters (e.g., earthquakes, floods, landslides, etc.)
- Accidents. For example, experiencing a road accident can cause fear about driving or getting into a vehicle. One of my friends got in an accident years ago. To date, being on the road still makes her anxious.

- Acts of terrorism (e.g., school shootings, bombings, hijackings, etc.) Terrorist activities of this sort are bound to leave anyone feeling scared and traumatized.
- Personal assaults (e.g., physical, mental, emotional, or sexual abuse)
- Losing a loved one. This may be the loss of a parental figure, sibling, relative, a dear friend, or anyone to whom you're close.
- Being diagnosed with a terminal or life-threatening illness. For example, imagine going to the doctor for a simple cough only to learn that a major illness is lying underneath. Suddenly, your whole world is upside down.
- Criminal activities (e.g., robbery, theft, kidnapping, etc.)

PTSD Symptoms

After a traumatic event, it can take up to three months before you start to feel the effects of PTSD. However, it's also possible to not experience any symptoms until many years later.

Also, the severity and duration of these symptoms can differ for each person. Some people have symptoms for more than a month and get better within six months; for some, getting better can take years.

PTSD symptoms are divided into four main types:

1. Reliving the Trauma Symptoms

These are also called *intrusion symptoms*. People with PTSD tend to get stuck on the traumatic event's memory and relive it repeatedly in their minds. Because of this, their minds are always in *alert mode*. Reliving the memory keeps them on their toes and keeps them from going through the same thing again. However, constantly thinking about a traumatic event causes a lot of distress, which can include:

- Nightmares
- Scary thoughts
- Flashbacks
- Hallucinations

2. Avoidance Symptoms

People with PTSD often try to deflect and deny the traumatic event. They might act like it didn't happen. But you can only hide for so long, and the trauma resurfaces sooner or later.

People under this PTSD category might stay away from places, people, things, and activities that remind them of the trauma. This can make it hard to stay close to family and friends, leading to isolation. This separation can also make someone stop doing things they used to enjoy. For example, someone who used to enjoy painting with their partner may stop if they suddenly lose their significant other.

Other examples of avoidance symptoms include:

- Not wanting to talk about the event;
- Canceling plans with friends and family; and
- Not caring about old hobbies and interests.

3. Emotional Arousal Symptoms

This PTSD category is for people who exhibit strong reactions, often negatively. For example, they may easily get angry, shout or throw things. The increased emotions also have other effects on the body, such as:

- Irritability

- Outbursts of anger
- Agitation
- Annoyance
- Trouble sleeping
- Difficulty focusing
- Hypersensitivity
- Tension and anxiety
- Fast, shallow breathing
- Tense muscles
- Nausea
- Diarrhea
- Lack of concentration

4. Cognitive Symptoms

Negative ideas about oneself or the world constitute cognitive symptoms. This can include:

- Guilt and shame
- Feelings of self-blame
- Feeling disconnected from others
- Feeling emotionally numb
- Loss of interest in life
- Depression and anxiety
- Developing phobias

Keep in mind that PTSD symptoms can also affect your *physical* health. That is, PTSD can show up in different ways in the body:

- Heavy sweating
- Trembling

- Dizziness
- Chest pains
- Stomach problems
- Headaches
- Weakened immune system

When these physical symptoms aren't taken care of, they can cause long-term changes in how a person behaves. For example, a weakened immune system makes people with PTSD prone to illness; heavy sweating and trembling may make young adults avoid others, leading to isolation and even drinking and drug use.

Adolescents aren't the only ones who can be affected by a traumatic event. Even children can get traumatized by terrible things, leaving them with PTSD symptoms.

For younger children, PTSD can slow down the development of their primary skills like talking, using the toilet, walking, and other motor skills. PTSD symptoms in children under six can include:

- Trouble speaking
- Playing out the event and reliving it by acting it out
- Wetting the bed
- Being too attached to an adult

Younger children may draw, tell stories, or make pictures to show how they feel. Since they can be more irritable and have communication issues due to their limited vocabulary, it's harder for them to make friends.

A coworker once told me this story about a very young child who has PTSD:

"I think he was only 4 years old when his mother died. She had cancer and got treatment on and off for a long time before she passed away. After she died, the child became quiet and wouldn't talk to anyone. His father was upset and had no idea what to do. He signed the child up for an arts camp because he liked to draw. After a few lessons, the art teacher told his father what he had learned.

The kid could only draw ambulances when he sat down to draw. When they talked to a child psychologist, they discovered this was the child's way of showing sadness. He was standing on the porch when an ambulance took his mother to the hospital, and she died there and never came back."

It might be hard for a child to tell an adult what they are feeling because they are still learning how to talk. So it helps to listen to what is not being said and watch for clues in their body language.

Reports also show that young adults are abused physically and sexually at a high rate, often leading to PTSD. It can have a big effect on the teen and lead to the following:

- Aggressive body language and mannerisms
- Self-harm
- Misuse of drugs to dull the pain
- Unusual or irregular sexual desires
- Low self-worth and self-esteem
- Feelings of fear and intense sadness

DBT for PTSD

"Trauma is personal. It does not disappear if it is not validated. When it is ignored or invalidated the silent screams continue internally heard only by the one held captive. When someone enters the pain and hears the screams healing can begin."
— Danielle Bernock

Now that we know more about PTSD let's find out how we can use DBT to cope with it and live better.

DBT can help to lessen the effects of PTSD and its symptoms. For one, it encourages you to recognize and deal with your trauma. This is important because suppressing the trauma can cause PTSD to manifest in other ways. For example, a teen who has lost a parent might start skipping school, getting into fights, or using drugs instead of dealing with their sadness.

We can use DBT Mindfulness techniques to stay in the present (as opposed to reliving the past traumatic event). Deep breathing can help calm your nervous system, making you feel better by bringing your attention to your thoughts, feelings, and surroundings in the present moment.

Worksheet: 4-7-8 Breathing

This exercise is an advanced breathing technique to reduce stress and anxiety.

Find a comfortable position.

INHALE for 4 counts through your nose.

| 1 | 2 | 3 | 4 |

HOLD YOU BREATH for 7 counts...

| 1 | 2 | 3 | 4 | 5 | 6 | 7 |

EXHALE for 8 counts through your mouth.

| 1 | 2 | 3 | 4 | 5 | 6 | 7 | 8 |

Do this for 4 times.

Remember, consistency is important! So please do breathing practice 2x daily for 4 weeks.

We can also use DBT Emotion Regulation techniques. This skill aims to help you understand and control your emotions instead of letting them control you.

With PTSD, it's easy to dwell on negative ways of thinking, deny the trauma or prevent reliving it. It's like going down a rabbit hole. But with emotion regulation skills, you can stop yourself from sliding down that hole.

One particular DBT emotion regulation exercise people with PTSD can try is called *Check the Facts*. When facing overwhelming emotion, this exercise will help you look at the facts to reduce the intensity of your extreme emotions.

Worksheet: Check the Facts

Use this worksheet to pause, reflect, and fact-check your feelings, helping you make sense of the situation and not overreact.

Question: What's the emotion you want to check? How intense is your emotion right now?

Example: my severe anxiety, emotion intensity level: 90

Your answer:

Emotion I want to fact-check: _____

Current emotion intensity level (0-100): _____

Question: What happened? What triggered this emotion?

Example: A birthday party of one of my friends is coming up, and I know that a group of kids who used to bully me will be there.

Your answer:

Question: What assumptions am I making about this trigger?

Example: They will bully me again.

Your answer:

CHECK THE FACTS! You listed your assumptions above, but <u>WHAT ELSE</u> can happen? List as many other possibilities as you can.

Example: (1) They may not bully me at all. (2) Some time has passed; maybe they've grown up a bit and are not even bullies anymore.

Your answer:

Question: Why am I reacting this way? What am I afraid of?

Example: I'm afraid I'll be embarrassed and be the night's joke.

Question: In the event what you're afraid of happens, list ways to cope with the situation.

Example: (1) I'll leave the party early at the first sign of bullying. (2) I'll call someone to pick me up, so I'm not alone.

Your answer:

Question: Does my emotion and its intensity fit the facts?
(0 = not at all to 5 = I am certain):

If you're not sure, keep looking at the facts. Be as creative as possible, ask other people what they think, or try something out to see if your ideas or predictions are right.

Example: Not sure.

Your answer:

After completing the above worksheet, what's your emotion intensity level now?

(0-100): _____

At the end of *Check the Facts*, your emotion intensity level should be lower than when you started. If not, please do the exercise again and remember to state only FACTS, not assumptions, opinions, or judgments.

Worksheet: Opposite to Emotion

After doing *Check the Facts* above, you may realize that you may be overreacting (i.e., the facts of the situation do not fit the emotion you're feeling). However, even though you realize this, you may still feel the same. So, this exercise helps you change that emotion and stop feeling that way.

Below is a table of emotions and a responding common urge. Write an opposing action to this natural tendency.

Emotion *What you're feeling.*	Emotion-Driven Behavior *What you would normally want to do because of this emotion. (If your natural urge is to do something other than what's listed below, list them on a separate sheet.)*	Opposite Action *Write down an opposite action to what you're feeling.*
Sadness	Self-isolation	Call a few friends and meet up with friends.
Guilt	Shutting down, self-criticism	
Anger	Shouting, sulking	
Fear	Running away from a situation	
Emptiness	Binge eating	
Loneliness	Getting back together with a toxic ex	

Emotion *What you're feeling.*	Emotion-Driven Behavior *What you would normally want to do because of this emotion. (If your natural urge is to do something other than what's listed below, list them on a separate sheet.)*	Opposite Action *Write down an opposite action to what you're feeling.*
Frustration	Throwing things around the room	
Helplessness	Crying and feeling depressed	
Resentment	Talking ill about someone/something	
Feel free to add more emotions and scenarios on the extra rows below.		

More Advice on How to Cope with PTSD

Getting better starts with taking care of yourself. It allows you to acknowledge your trauma and take steps to improve your situation. The goal is to make small changes over time to lessen the effects of PTSD and make your life better. Remember these things as you get better:

- Get a good understanding of PTSD and what caused yours.
- Realize that recovery takes time.
- Understand that healing is not linear but a slow, winding process.
- Learn how DBT tools can help with your PTSD.

"We don't heal alone; we heal as a group."
— S. Kelley Harrell

As you move forward, focus on maintaining a supportive group of people around you. You can do the following:

1. **Tell your parents, teachers, and friends what you want and how you feel.** For example, tell a friend if you want to spend more time with them. If you need help with a project from your teacher, tell them.

2. **Spend time with people who are like you.** For example, if you have an open mind and don't judge people, hang out with people who are also open-minded and nonjudgmental. This will help you feel at ease, thus lessening your daily stress. In contrast, hanging out with negative people or those who don't value or accept you, will just make you feel bad and add to your stress.

3. **Find a group of people with PTSD who can help you.** This helps you feel like you belong and are part of a group. You can find groups and

communities on Facebook that are good for this purpose. Local centers offer psychotherapy support groups as well, so check them out.

4. **Tell other people what sets you off** so they can be aware. For example, if you get upset when people drive too fast or talk about a certain event, let your friends know so they can be a bit more mindful about what they discuss with you.

5. **Engage in physical activities** like exercise, swimming, running, etc. Physical activities make people happier and less stressed out. I recommend working out thrice a week for at least 30 minutes daily. Yoga and resistance bands are my favorite ways to work out.

6. Do things like **breathing exercises and meditation to help you feel more stable**. You can start by doing these for 10 minutes, and as you get better, you can add more time. Deep breathing exercises help your nervous system in so many ways.

7. **Do things that make you happy**, like working out, going on hikes, painting, yoga, etc. Think about your favorite interests and hobbies and try to do them at least twice or thrice a week.

8. **Spend time with nature.** Parks and other open places where you can see greenery and clear blue skies can help you relax.

Just keep in mind that you are not alone on this journey. Healing takes time, and challenges are ahead, but I'm here for you. But more importantly, you're here for yourself.

Chapter 7: OCD & Compulsive Behaviors

"You're helpless to the behavior but the effort involved is just unbelievable."
— Patrick Ness

Getting Personal: My OCD Life

This quote above resonates well with me. When I think about how hard it was for me to deal with OCD, I wish I had known what I know now. I wouldn't have felt so helpless if I had understood what was happening to me. Even though I've always had anxiety, my OCD didn't get out of hand until I was in high school.

I couldn't start my day until I did my daily routines, which often took me more than an hour. I usually stayed up until 3 or 4 AM on the weekends because I knew I would have to do the same things the next day. It was my way of delaying the inevitable. The mere thought of having to go through my daily compulsions depressed me. And yet, I could not stop.

My eating and sleeping habits were terrible, and I often ate snacks late at night to comfort myself. Because I couldn't get up on time, I was often late to school. I didn't have enough energy or focus, so I would sleep in the library during lunch to make up for it.

The hardest thing was that I didn't know what was happening. I knew it wasn't "normal," but I was too scared to tell anyone about it.

As my OCD worsened, I started doing more compulsive things, like turning the tap on and off and turning the lights on and off. I would always check the stove and locks before leaving the house to ensure the home was safe. I took longer showers because I wanted to ensure that every part of my body was clean.

Even walking outside was hard because I had to be careful not to step on certain lines on the pavement so that "something bad" wouldn't happen. I would even skip some tiles because they were thought to be "unlucky." My obsessions and compulsions were causing a lot of trouble in my life.

The strange thing is that I knew it wasn't normal behavior. However, despite my best efforts, I couldn't stop myself from performing my compulsions. I felt I had to do them because some internal force made me.

Fortunately, things gradually improved, especially since I started applying DBT techniques. I still have mild OCD and will probably always have it, but it is much more manageable now. Once I realized I was dealing with a condition and that there wasn't anything "wrong" with me, I felt a huge weight lifted off my shoulders. There was finally hope!

I wish I could say that my OCD symptoms just disappeared, but that never happens. I had to work hard and spend a lot of time understanding my condition, what was causing it, and how to address it.

Once I started to radically accept my condition (yes, thanks to DBT), I could finally open up to others. Consequently, I came into contact with other people with OCD, and learning about their experiences helped me. It made me feel less lonely and isolated. If you're struggling with OCD, I hope reading my experiences will help you too.

What Is OCD?

Obsessions and compulsions are the two main aspects of obsessive-compulsive disorder (OCD), a mental illness.

Ruminating and fixating are characteristics of an *obsession*, which refers to recurring, unwanted thoughts and behaviors. An urge or impulse to do something repeatedly is a *compulsion*. Some people have obsessions or compulsions, while others have both.

It's not a sign of OCD to bite your nails or occasionally experience unhappy feelings. It goes further than that. For instance, OCD can involve the idea that only particular actions or things are right or wrong. The obsessive aspect of OCD causes a black-and-white perspective. You don't want to think or feel this way, but you feel helpless to change. Once you experience a particular thought (*obsession*), it compels you to act to feel better (*compulsion*).

In my case, I had to repeatedly turn the tap on and off to avoid a bad situation. Washing your hands repeatedly after touching something unclean is another common compulsion.

OCD thoughts and actions exhibit the following traits:

- They take up more than an hour of your day.
- They are uncontrollable.
- They don't offer any pleasure or enjoyment
- They affect your social, professional, and personal life.

One of my readers, the eldest of five daughters, wrote me an email describing her recent difficulties. I've included it here with her consent to demonstrate how OCD can affect your life.

"I feel helpless. My dad travels a lot for work, so I'm constantly concerned for him. Sometimes, he and his colleagues are in the middle of nowhere. I'm so afraid that he might suffer some harm. I'm not just constantly worried about him but other family members as well. I constantly fear someone breaking into the house and harming us.

So, I must ensure the doors are properly locked before I can sleep at night. To feel secure, I must repeatedly inspect them, and I must also repeatedly check the light switches to ensure nobody is there. I occasionally get the urge to check on everyone at home in the middle of the night to ensure they are all still in their beds."

Fortunately, her dad is unharmed, and her family is fine. But you can see that she's showing OCD symptoms. These consist of:

- Repeatedly checking up on loved ones.
- Repetitively checking house lights.
- Constantly inspecting door locks.

These symptoms do not automatically mean she has OCD, but they are indications that she might.

How OCD Shows Up

Although there are many kinds of OCD, it has four main categories:

1. **Inspection:** constantly checking things like locks, taps, alarm clocks, electricity switches, stoves, etc., is a part of this.

2. **Symmetry**: wanting things to be just right or flawless. Arranging and aligning objects a certain way is a compulsion and may also entail stroking and touching things.

3. **Contamination:** worrying excessively about getting sick or spreading germs. You try to cope with this extreme worry and distress by constantly cleaning, such as handwashing and taking showers.

4. **Rumination:** having disruptive, intrusive thoughts. For example, this might involve having constant perfectionist thoughts or engaging in inappropriate behaviors. It may also make you avoid certain areas to stay clean or ensure you haven't hurt or harmed anyone.

DBT for OCD

DBT focuses on positively altering thought patterns to facilitate behavior change. It can help treat pain, fears, and stressors that seep into everyday life when having OCD.

DBT puts a heavy emphasis on building unconditional self-acceptance and a non-judgmental, safe space within yourself. People with OCD learn to trust themselves and their surroundings in a therapeutic setting. It encourages you to be open and honest about your thoughts and emotions and discourages dwelling on negative feelings of guilt and shame or thinking that something is wrong with you.

DBT acknowledges your efforts to accept and talk about your struggles and progress. Opening up can be scary for a lot of people. Establishing trust with a therapist is important for people attending therapy since it promotes acceptance and change by encouraging patients to confront their obsessions and compulsions.

Note, though, that if you're trying DBT on your own, you can still benefit by learning about it and doing the exercises in this book.

Emotion Regulation and **Distress Tolerance** are two DBT skills that can have a tremendous positive impact on people with OCD.

Emotion Regulation

When it comes to emotions, we often think of just our *feelings*. However, there is a strong link between our minds and bodies.[18] In other words, having a healthy body and mind are related.

Worksheet: PLEASE

This DBT exercise emphasizes the importance of taking care of our physical health because an unhealthy body makes it difficult for us to manage our emotions.

PL Physical Illness

If you're physically unwell, don't hesitate to see a doctor and take any prescribed medications. If you're unable to see a physician, reach out to someone (e.g., a friend, a relative, a neighbor, etc.) so that you're not alone during this time. If you prefer alternative medicine or want to follow a holistic approach to wellness, that's ok too. The point is to seek help so that you don't stay physically ill.

When was the last time you were physically ill? _____

Did you see a doctor?   Y / N

Why or why not? _____

_____

E Balanced Eating

Ensure that you're eating a healthy, well-balanced diet. Avoid stress eating or emotional eating as these moments often make you want to grab something high in sugar, which is not good for your overall health.

Below is a short, 7-day food journal. Write down everything you eat and drink. At the end of the week, look at your food journal and see if you're consuming too much sugar (cookies, cake, soda, pastries, energy drinks, etc.), processed foods (food items that come out of a box), or junk foods (chips, candy, etc.).

Please do not overthink this; just write down what you eat and drink, review it at the end of seven (7) days and then slowly make better choices. For example, if you drink three cans of soda daily, change to just two cans. When you're used to that, cut to one can daily. When you're used to that, switch to water.

7-DAY FOOD LOG			
Day	Breakfast	Lunch	Dinner
Example:	*3 pancakes w/ 1 tbsp maple syrup; a banana; 1 glass of orange juice*	*At school: 1 serving mac n' cheese; 6 pcs chicken nuggets; 1 cookie; 1 small bottle of water*	*1.5 cups white rice; 2 pcs fried chicken; green beans; 1 small glass of soda*
Monday			
Tuesday			
Wednesday			
Thursday			

7-DAY FOOD LOG			
Day	Breakfast	Lunch	Dinner
Friday			
Saturday			
Sunday			

Are you eating healthily? Consuming healthy meals at regular intervals keeps you satiated throughout the day. Opt for 4-6 smaller meals instead of a large lunch and dinner to keep you properly fueled. A few healthy food options include:

- Nuts and seeds because they are rich in nutrients.
- Protein-rich food, for example, eggs, beans, and meat.
- Complex carbohydrates like fruits, fresh vegetables, and whole grains keep your blood sugar balanced.

Proper nutrition is vital to your mental health recovery. However, it's a broad subject that's beyond the scope of this book. As such, I encourage you to talk your doctor or a nutritionist to receive proper and customized nutritional advice.

People with OCD should restrict caffeine consumption because it can elevate anxiety levels. If you must have coffee or tea, limit yourself to one cup by noon.

Caffeine stays in the body for roughly 5 hours. However, it can linger in the body for 9.5 hours. Instead of coffee, try herbal tea instead, especially at night.

A Avoid Unhealthy Substances

As a teen, this is when you'll probably be exposed to illegal drugs and alcohol for the first time. Avoid taking these as they can worsen your OCD.

S Sleep

Adolescents should regularly sleep for 8-10 hours.[19] If you're not getting this much sleep, your energy levels will be low, and your ability to regulate your emotion will be impaired.

7-DAY SLEEP LOG			
	Sleep Time	**Wake Time**	**Total Sleep Hours**
Example:	*11:30 PM*	*6:00 AM*	*6.5 hours*
Monday			
Tuesday			
Wednesday			
Thursday			
Friday			
Saturday			
Sunday			

Are you sleeping enough? If not, a good sleep routine will help you clock in more sleep hours. Here are some tips for you.

1. At least an hour before bedtime, turn off your screens. Blue light from our screens prevents melatonin production, the hormone that makes us feel sleepy. A good place to start is to use an app such as _Twilight_ for your phone, or _f.lux_ for your laptop. These apps change the color of your device's display screen, adapting them to the time of day.

2. Meditation, light yoga, and deep breathing can help your body make more melatonin and calm you down before bed.

3. Do something relaxing before bed, such as listening to calming music or reading a book.

4. Turn down the room's noise and light.

5. Cool down the room. Room temperatures between 60 and 67°F improve the quality of REM sleep.

6. Get into a warm bath. Researchers have found that taking a hot bath 1 to 2 hours before bed can help you fall asleep faster by lowering your body's core temperature.

E Exercise

Try to get in at least 30 minutes of active movement daily. If you haven't worked out in a while, start with something shorter, like 10 minutes.

7-DAY EXERCISE LOG		
	Exercise Activity	**Time Spent**
Example:	*Swimming*	*1 hour*
Monday		
Tuesday		
Wednesday		
Thursday		
Friday		
Saturday		
Sunday		

Are you exercising enough? Y / N

If not, list down ways to increase your active hours.

Example: wake up earlier than normal to jog, take the stairs instead of the elevator, join mom/dad at the gym, etc.

1.	
2.	
3.	
4.	
5.	

Stress and worry cause the body to make a hormone called *cortisol*. It's good in small amounts for short periods but bad when it stays high for a long time.

Adding movement and exercise to your daily routine keeps your mental and physical health and cortisol levels in check. Yoga, jogging, walking, swimming, and resistance training are good ways to move.

Distress Tolerance

Distress tolerance skills teach you how to withstand negative emotions, and it's an important skill to have in your arsenal when dealing with OCD.[20] The following DBT exercise—**TIPP**—teaches you how to tolerate moments when you feel overwhelmed by your OCD. It will help you cope with distressing feelings, reduce the intensity of your obsessions and compulsions, and help release any emotional build-up.

Worksheet: TIPP

Temperature: Make yourself feel better by putting something cold on your face. You can turn on the tap and splash your face with cold water, put your head in the fridge for a few seconds, or just go outside when it's cold.

Intense Exercise: Relax your body by doing vigorous exercise. Sometimes, a brief 7-minute routine is all that is required. If you're truly pressed for time, even 5 minutes is enough! For example, you can use the _5 Minute Home Workouts_ app by Olson Applications to get in some quick movement during the day. The key is to keep going until your intense feelings start to fade.

Paced Breathing: Thoughts and emotions racing? Slow down by taking slow, deep breaths in and out. For example, take 4 seconds to breathe in and 5 seconds to breathe out.

Paired Muscle Relaxation: Do this while you are doing Paced Breathing up above. As you take a deep breath in, slowly tense your muscles (but not so much that they cramp), and as you take a deep breath out, let all that tension go and tell yourself, "Relax."

More Advice on How to Cope with OCD

In addition to the DBT skill exercises above, here are a few more tips on better handling your OCD.

1. **Be open to receiving support.** You shouldn't feel bad about asking for help; it doesn't make you weak. When people back you up, it's much easier to be successful. Start by discussing your symptoms and problems with people you care about, such as a close family member. If you're uncomfortable with this, inform your parent(s), teacher, counselor, or any trusted authority figure that you want to see a therapist. The support of others will make things easier for you and help people understand your situation better. You can also join a group with other OCD sufferers. You can do this by visiting a support center or by joining an online group. Facebook and Reddit are examples of social networks with OCD-focused support groups.

2. **Find time to unwind.** Even though it sounds like a cliché, it's important to slow down and take it easy. We're always thinking about everything we need to do, so we often forget to care for ourselves. Take some time for yourself every day, even if it's just 5 minutes. Find a place that is quiet where you won't be easily disturbed. Close your eyes and take some deep breaths to calm down. Yoga, meditation, walking or strolling in nature, painting, etc., are other things you can do. Do something that makes you happy and brings you peace.

3. **Get the right medication.** Even though medications aren't right for everyone, they can be very helpful for the right people. I used to be against medications, but the truth is that I felt less anxious when I started taking them. I now understand that medicines are just another way to help you

get better. The key is not to depend on them but to use them along with therapy to help you deal with your obsessions and compulsions.

4. **Rejoice in small victories.** It can be hard to come to terms with OCD and learn how to live with it. You must be willing to self-reflect and take the necessary steps to get better. Keep a journal of your progress and write down any changes, no matter how small.

Chapter 8: Eating Disorders

"I am forever engaged in a silent battle in my head over whether or not to lift the fork to my mouth, and when I talk myself into doing so, I taste only shame. I have an eating disorder."
— Jena Morrow

I never had a serious eating disorder, but I had an odd way of eating when I was younger. My obsessions and compulsions would change from time to time because I have OCD. But when I was a young teen, I felt like I couldn't swallow until I had chewed my food a certain number of times.

I sometimes spit out food when I ate (I know, gross). I thought that if I did that, it would stop something bad from happening to me. I stopped doing this over time. Finally, I could enjoy my food without having to chew it a certain number of times or throw it back up.

What Is an Eating Disorder?

Eating disorders include a variety of mental conditions that cause undesirable eating patterns. People with this disorder might start with being obsessed with food or their body weight, shape, or size. People of all ages, races, ethnicities, body weights, and genders can have eating disorders. But young adults are more likely to have them, especially young women. Data shows that up to 13% of teens and young adults will have at least one type of eating disorder by age 20.[21]

People with eating disorders can display various symptoms, including food restriction, extreme overeating, or cleansing practices like vomiting or excessive exercising.

In severe cases, eating disorders can cause health problems that, if left untreated for a long time, can lead to death. For example, a person with *anorexia nervosa* may not eat because they are worried about their weight. Over time, this can cause a person to be severely underweight, hungry, tired, and weak. If they keep going in this direction, their extreme eating habits may lead to an early death.

What Causes Eating Disorders?

Various biological, behavioral, psychological, and social factors can contribute to eating disorders.

Biological Factors. Young adults with a family history of illnesses or conditions are more prone to developing unhealthy eating habits. Medication for depression and anxiety can increase the risks of developing an eating disorder. Eating disorders like anorexia, bulimia and binge eating are more common in people with diabetes.

Psychological Factors. Certain personality traits can increase your risk of developing an eating disorder, such as perfectionism, low self-esteem, poor body image, and impulsiveness. A traumatic experience also makes it likely to develop an eating disorder.

Environmental/Social Factors. Environmental factors include your family, friends, and society. It also includes your culture's views on food and body image standards. What may be desirable in one culture may be undesirable in another. These factors play an important role in shaping your self-image and whether you will develop an eating disorder.

"To lose confidence in one's body is to lose confidence in oneself."
— *Simone de Beauvoir*

Eating Disorder Symptoms

Eating disorders are complicated and can impact your mental, physical, and emotional health. Let's look at some possible symptoms to better understand whether you have an eating disorder.

Emotional/Behavioral Symptoms. Eating disorders can affect both your mood and behaviors, such as:

- Being preoccupied with dieting and weight loss
- Frequent mood swings
- Always checking yourself in the mirror
- Dissatisfaction with your body
- Withdrawing emotionally from others
- Shying away from social interactions, especially those involving food
- Avoiding others while eating
- Constantly checking calories and nutritional content
- Preoccupation with weighing yourself
- Skipping meals often
- Feeling shame and guilt about eating or weight gain

Physical Symptoms. Unsurprisingly, eating disorders impact your physical health negatively. Symptoms include the following.

- Visible fluctuations in weight gain or loss
- Gastrointestinal problems, such as constipation
- Slow heart rate
- Low blood pressure
- Brittle hair and nails
- Pale or dry skin
- Dizziness or fainting

- Fatigue and tiredness
- Irregular menstrual cycles
- Thinning or having brittle hair
- Weak muscles
- Weak immune system

If you think you might have an eating disorder, please talk to your parent, guardian, or doctor for help.

DBT for Eating Disorders

"Even the models we see in magazines wish they could look like their own images."

— **Cheri K. Erdman**

Interpersonal Effectiveness

As mentioned above, environmental and social factors are some of the causes of eating disorders. Sometimes, we turn to food because there's no one we can turn to in times of distress. Food becomes our solace. Food, not people, gives us comfort.

So, one of the ways we can heal from an eating disorder is to work on our *interpersonal effectiveness*, which is our ability to interact with others successfully.

For example, say you are on a health and fitness journey, but your family and friends do not support you. It may be hard to stay true to your health plan because they constantly tempt you with food even though you explicitly tell them not to do that. DBT interpersonal effectiveness skills will help you communicate your wants and needs so that other people will listen and respect them.

But of course, it's not all one-sided. Others should also feel that you are someone who can understand and hear them too. DBT interpersonal effectiveness skills help you find that balance.

Worksheet: FAST

Sometimes, you might betray your values and beliefs in relationships to receive approval or get what you want. The FAST exercise below will help you achieve self-respect effectiveness.

 air.

Be reasonable when communicating your wants and needs. Stick to the facts and avoid emotional and dramatic outbursts.

Example: I'm trying to eat healthier. Please don't bake cookies for me.

Not: Oh my God! Why are you sabotaging my health?!

Your Turn: What do you want to ask? What's your request?

A pologies are not necessary.

Don't apologize for your request. Remember that you have a right to ask for it; the only time to apologize is if you've done something wrong. Also, the more assertive you are with your request, the more the other person will take you seriously.

Example: I've decided to eat healthier, so can we please have more fruit and vegetables at home?

NOT: I'm sorry! I know it's so inconvenient for you to buy fruit and vegetables when I'm the only one eating most of them.

Your Turn: Practice requesting something without apologizing for it.

S tick to your values.

Don't compromise just because the other person is not comfortable or does not want to give in to your request. This is especially true if doing the opposite of your request goes against your values.

Your Turn: List down 3 things you will not compromise on.

Examples: eating junk food, drinking energy drinks, skipping meals

1)

2)

3)

T ruthfulness.

Don't lie or exaggerate to get what you want.

Example: I don't like you talking to our other friends about what and how I eat. Please stop.

Not: Why did you talk to our friends about what and how I eat? How could you? It's so embarrassing! I'll never be able to look them in the eye again.

Your Turn: Write down a request and try to just stick to the facts. Avoid judgments, lies, or exaggerations.

Emotion Regulation

A lot of eating disorders emerge from an inability to manage emotions. I'm no stranger to this. As I mentioned earlier, I turned heavily to junk food to deal with my mental health problems and all the emotional turmoil they brought.

Emotional regulation differs from distress tolerance. Distress tolerance teaches us how to *tolerate* or cope with an unpleasant moment; emotion regulation teaches us to find the most effective way to *manage* high emotions.

By learning how to regulate our feelings during highly stressful moments, we can refrain from falling into damaging eating behaviors, such as binge eating or starving.

Worksheet: What Else?

Do this DBT exercise whenever you feel like turning to food for emotional comfort.

Step 1: What emotion do you want to change? On a scale from 1-10, what intensity is the emotion?

Example: Extreme sadness; intensity 8

Your turn:

Emotion: _____

Intensity (1-10): _____

Step 2: What do you want to do because of this emotion? What's your 'urge'?

Example: I want to skip meals.

Your turn:

_____

_____

_____

Step 3: What triggered this emotion? Describe the situation that caused this emotion. Be as detailed as possible.

Example: My one and only friend at school is sick and won't be in for a week. I'm so anxious to be alone.

Your turn:

_____

_____

_____

Step 4: Understand your emotional reaction. Is this the ONLY thing that can happen? List down all OTHER possibilities. (WHAT ELSE can happen?)

Example: (1) Maybe my best friend would come back earlier. (2) I've been looking at this club I want to join, maybe I should do that now and make new friends.

Your turn:

_____

_____

_____

Step 5: Re-evaluate your emotion. Now that you've taken a step back and thought about OTHER possibilities (what else), is your emotion intensity still high?

If yes, take a break and do step 4 again.

If not, go ahead and do *something else* than your original urge. List down what you want to do.

Example: take a walk, listen to feel-good music, grab an apple (instead of skipping a meal, bingeing or turning to junk food.

Your turn:

_____

_____

_____

More Advice on How to Cope with an Eating Disorder

In addition to the DBT skill exercises above, here are a few more tips on how to get better from an eating disorder.

Keep a mood and food diary. Keep a diary to track what you eat and how you feel at any given time. It will help you figure out your 'triggers'.

Develop a healthy relationship with food. Many people with eating disorders tend to see food as 'good', so they tend to eat more, or as 'bad', so they tend to avoid it at all costs. Instead, try not to be judgmental of food. Think of it as a source of energy for your body. And if you want a healthy body, you need to give it healthy fuel.

And don't judge yourself either. Give yourself permission to eat the foods you enjoy and curtail consumption of foods you know harm your body. Also, shift away from calorie obsession and focus first on being friends with food again.

Support. A great support system can make a huge difference. Having someone to talk to or turn to for support motivates you during difficult times. If you fall off the bandwagon, you can turn to your group for support (instead of food) to help you get back on track.

Exercise. Many eating disorders are linked to body image issues. However, instead of focusing on food intake, take physical activities instead. Exercise improves your mood by releasing endorphins in your brain. The better you feel, the less likely you are to over- or under eat. Exercise creates a positive body image, reduces stress, and regulates anxiety. Run, walk, swim, and dance around your living room. It does not need to be structured, and it does not need to be intense and difficult. Just ensure that you are moving!

Sleep. Poor sleeping habits impact your eating as well. When you are tired, you feel cranky, and to overcome this, you eat mindlessly. Aim for 7-8 hours of sleep every night. Rest!

Chapter 9: Self-Harm

*"The only person who can pull me down is myself,
and I'm not going to let myself pull me down anymore."*
- C. JoyBell C.

Getting Personal: My Struggles with Self-Harm

Coming across this quote on the internet made me think back on one of my all-time favorite movies, Terminator 2. If you're unfamiliar, it's a 90s sci-fi action movie that stars Arnold Schwarzenegger as a T-800, a cybernetic machine from the future. The T-800 is sent to the present time to protect a young John Connor from getting killed by another Terminator, the T-1000.

The T-1000 is sent by Skynet, an advanced AI computer system that becomes self-aware and views humanity as a threat to its existence. As a result, Skynet starts a nuclear war that kills most of human civilization. John Connor is one of the few remaining human survivors and ultimately leads the human resistance to defeat Skynet.

In one scene, John and the T-800 are fixing their broken car when they notice two young boys playing with their toy guns and arguing about who killed each other first.

John turns to the T-800 and says, *"We're not gonna make it, are we? People, I mean."* The Terminator replies, *"It's in your nature to destroy yourselves."*

You can watch the scene here:

https://tinyurl.com/t2scene

To this day, this line rings true to me. On more than one occasion, I thought about what it would feel like to jump off my 17th-floor balcony and see what would happen. Would I survive? Would I be paralyzed? What would my final thoughts be before hitting the ground? Would others even care?

If you have thought about harming yourself or tried, realize you're not alone. Life's confusing and tough, especially during your teenage years. You're going through many changes and constantly under pressure from family, friends, and school. At the same time, you're trying to figure out who you are as a person while trying to fit in with your peers.

In school, being "cool" meant wearing Nike gear. If you didn't have Nike, you weren't considered cool and seen as an outcast. This expectation created a lot of pressure to wear brand-name clothes (often expensive) to impress my schoolmates. My parents didn't have money for these things since they had to be used for more important matters, such as paying for food and electricity. Wearing brand-name clothes wasn't at the top of priorities.

As a result, I always felt that I didn't belong. This added to my anxiety, which made me feel depressed and entertain thoughts about self-harm.

Understanding Self-Harm

Self-harm is any behavior or action you do that causes harm or pain to you. Self-harm is a way to deal with painful thoughts, feelings, and situations. Most of the time, people who harm themselves do it for the following reasons:

- Express their struggles and pain to others.
- Turn emotional pain into a more tangible, physical pain.
- Gain a sense of self-control.
- Distract from troubling thoughts and feelings.
- Escape trauma.

- Punish themselves because they feel shame or guilt.
- Deal with feelings of numbness; to feel connected somehow.
- Redirect suicidal thoughts without taking their own life.

Self-harm can include:

- Poisoning
- Cutting yourself
- Over-eating, under-eating or starving
- Excessive workouts
- Scratching your skin
- Burning your skin
- Biting yourself
- Pulling your hair
- Indulging in unsafe sexual activities
- Abusing drugs, such as alcohol and prescribed and recreational medications
- Hitting yourself or punching the wall
- Starting fights to get beaten up by others

The Cycle of Self-harm

Self-harm can be a vicious cycle. As mentioned, one common reason why people harm themselves is to gain a sense of self-control.

It often starts with stressful thoughts and feelings, so you physically hurt yourself to stop feeling the emotional pain. However, guilt and shame take over when the short-term relief is gone. When you feel so guilty that you can't take it anymore, you start hurting yourself again to get rid of the pain. As you do this over and over, hurting yourself becomes a normal way of dealing with problems you face every day. This cycle will continue if you don't try to change your behavior for the better.

DBT for Self-Harm

"You have been criticizing yourself for years, and it hasn't worked. Try approving of yourself and see what happens."

-LOUISE L. HAY

Mindfulness

Mindfulness techniques enable struggling individuals to be more grounded. It brings self-harming thoughts and feelings as they arise into your cognitive awareness. It encourages you to practice compassion and accept these thoughts without judging or shaming yourself.

By giving space to these thoughts and acknowledging them, you allow them to just 'BE' (exist), and then you can release them. Accepting and releasing are better because suppression only makes them return later on in a more pronounced manner.

Mindfulness teaches us to be more compassionate towards ourselves. Our struggles don't define us; we CAN overcome them with the right tools and mindset.

"The real difficulty is to overcome how you think about yourself."

Studies have shown that mindfulness is effective when dealing with self-harm thoughts.[22,23]

DBT's "Wise Mind" is a mental state in which our rational and emotional minds meet and work together. It is a very important part of DBT. Wise Mind combines emotions and logic in a way that works. We can train ourselves to use our Wise Minds through regular reflection.

People who practice Wise Mind learn more about themselves, their instincts, and how they act. It helps you deal with the many things that happen in life in the best way possible. When we use Wise Mind in the things we do daily, it becomes a part of how we work. When you act from a place of wisdom, you feel less stress and anxiety and can better control your emotions.

Wise Mind also helps you self-regulate when a self-harming thought occurs. Taking a 5-minute break to do breathing exercises or mediate during a stressful day are examples of Wise Mind. It can also mean taking a break from a heated argument with your partner, a friend, or your parents and coming back to the situation with a clearer head.

Worksheet: Wise Mind

The Wise Mind exercise below will help ground you and prevent self-harming behaviors during difficult times.

This image illustrates Wise Mind.

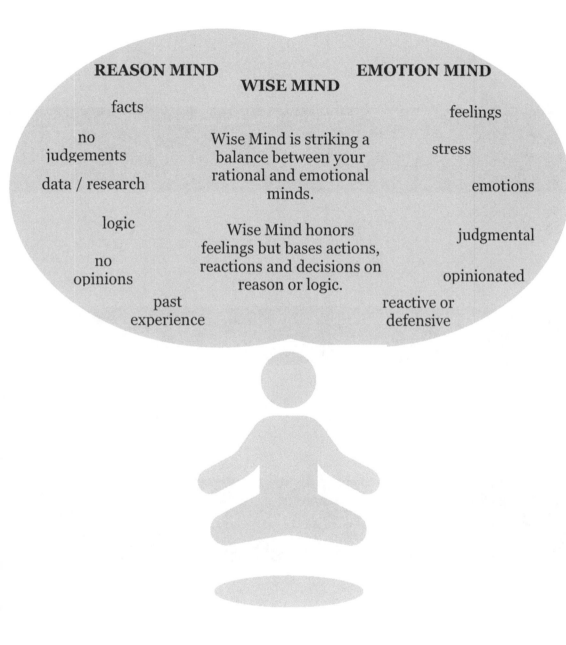

Keeping the above in mind, please answer the following questions.

Question: Think of a previous experience or situation where you regretted your reaction.
Example: A fight with my best friend, Emily.

Question: What happened? Be specific about the situation but don't offer any opinion or judgment. (Stick to the facts.)
Example: I learned that she shared a secret of mine with a mutual friend.

Question: What did you think, say or do?
Example: I was upset, but I called her right away and called her a snitch.

Question: Why do you regret this action?
Example: Because I found out later she didn't tell any secret, someone else did, and now she's taking her distance.

Question: If you had practiced **WISE MIND**, what would have happened?
Example: I would have checked first if Emily did tell my secret. Till then, I should have given her the benefit of the doubt since she's never spilled a secret of mine before. I wouldn't have called and made unfounded accusations. If I had followed Wise Mind, I would still have my best friend beside me right now.

Emotion Regulation

Managing your emotions is a useful and life-changing skill. As we've already seen, thoughts and actions that hurt oneself happen after strong feelings. If you want to break out of the cycle of self-harm, you must learn how to handle your feelings. The goal is to keep the feelings from getting out of hand. Problems appear when emotions blow out of proportion and are left unattended.

After you've learned how to be mindful (Mindfulness) and deal with stress (Distress Tolerance), it's easier to learn how to control your emotions (Emotion Regulation). The shift starts to happen when you take a mindful pause between your thoughts and actions. This is where you learn to control your feelings and put self-love ahead of self-harm.

A 2018 study on how people deal with their emotions and self-harm found that *"poor emotion regulation was often given as a reason for self-harm."* This review looked at 17 different research papers and studies and found that emotional regulation made it more likely that people wouldn't hurt themselves.[24]

There is an inverse relationship between emotional regulation and self-harm. If you don't have enough emotional regulation, you may be more likely to hurt yourself. Studies show that when a person's ability to control their emotions is low, they are more likely to "lose their balance" during unpleasant emotional experiences and hurt themselves as a result.

Worksheet: Do the Opposite

This Emotion Regulation worksheet will help you improve at keeping your emotions in check when you're stressed or upset.

Following are some everyday situations in which you might find yourself. Write down what you usually do when these things happen. What are your thoughts when they happen? How do you feel or react? What do you do? Is there a better way you could handle that situation?

Scenario	Feeling	Thought	Behavior	Alternate Action
Your friend lied to you about talking to your ex after you broke up.	*I feel very angry, hurt, and depressed.*	*My friend betrayed me. Is she dating my ex? I feel so alone.*	*I lash out at her and give her the cold shoulder.* *I also want to hurt myself because I can't deal with the pain of my breaking up and my best friend betraying me.*	*First, I need to slow down. I'll call my friend and ask what happened.* *I'll do Distress Tolerance exercises (e.g., TIPP) to avoid self-harm.*
You worked hard to get an A on a test but got a C.				

Scenario	Feeling	Thought	Behavior	Alternate Action
Your best friend canceled your plans to meet up at the last minute.				
You went on a few dates with someone; you like them, and now they're ghosting you.				
Someone made fun of you on social media.				
Feel free to add more scenarios on the extra rows below.				

Scenario	Feeling	Thought	Behavior	Alternate Action

More Advice on What to Do When Thoughts of Self-Harm Occur

It can be hard to deal with self-harm thoughts and behavior. However, getting into healthier habits can help a lot to cut down on such self-destructive behavior. One of the best ways to get into good habits is to find something else to do when you want to hurt yourself. Depending on your personality and interests, there are many different kinds of distractions.

Journal your thoughts. Write down your feelings, especially when you're overwhelmed with negative emotions. Thinking of it as lashing put on paper. You still get to vent, but you're not harming any of your relationships

Write and shred. Write negative thoughts on a piece of paper and shred them. This allows you to release your thoughts into the physical world and serves as a good catharsis for your difficult emotions.

Use stress toys. Stress relief toys are good ways to take your mind off things and keep your hands busy. Stress balls or fidget spinners that you can squeeze or spin are good choices. Studies have shown that fidget spinners may help with anxiety because they are distracting, and you need to move them on purpose.

Practice mindful breathing. Breathing exercises like belly breathing and breathing through one nostril at a time can help you calm down. Headspace, Calm, and Simple Habit are all apps people like and recommend. (I'm using Simply Habit right now, and I love that there are so many guided meditations to choose from.) Ten minutes a day is a good goal.

Go outside and enjoy nature. Research shows that being in nature can help reduce stress and anxiety and help you calm down and relax tense muscles.

[25,26] Vitamin D, made by the sun, is important for your immune system. Try to get at least 10 to 15 minutes of sun whenever you can.

Call a friend, family member, or any loved one. Studies have shown that talking to a friend can help relieve stress. People are social animals, and we all want to be with other people. Go through your contact list and see who you haven't talked to in a while. Call even if it's just for 5 minutes.

Create art. Drawing, painting, etc., is a way to show what's inside you. It lets you express your feelings through another medium. Spend some time doing something you enjoy that helps you stay on task.

Listen to 'pick me up' music. Listen to your favorite music. Studies have shown that classical and soft pop music can help calm your nervous system.[27]

Worksheet: JOY LIST

A JOY LIST is exactly what it means— a list of the things in your life that bring you happiness. Create this list so that you have a ready list of things to do to distract yourself and turn your mind (to positivity) when ideas of self-harm occur. We already put some samples below. Just fill out the rest of the list!

MY JOY LIST	
1. *Dance to my favorite heart-pumping tune.*	11.
2. *Look at pictures from a great vacation I had with family.*	12.
3. *Plan a picnic with my BFF.*	13.
4. *Talk to grandma.*	14.
5. *Go for a hike in nature.*	15.
6. *Do yoga.*	16.
7.	17.
8.	18.
9.	19.
10.	20.

Chapter 10: Boundaries

"NO is a complete sentence."
- Anne Lamont

You have the right to say "no" to anything that makes you feel uncomfortable; this is called setting boundaries, which most of us have trouble defining and claiming. I'm not saying you shouldn't help your mom with the dishes or take out the trash. I'm talking about setting non-defensive boundaries that make you feel safe in your relationships. Setting limits is not only okay, but it's important.

In this chapter, we'll discuss setting boundaries for your physical and emotional space. Someone touching you without permission or your parents walking into your room without knocking are examples of crossing your physical boundaries. Someone talking to you rudely, calling you selfish, or making you feel guilty because you don't do 'enough' for other people are examples of crossing your emotional boundaries.

Getting Personal: Boundary Issues in My Family

In Chinese culture, your elders are always right. Children who disobey or disagree with their parents are seen as defiant and ungrateful. This is known as filial piety.

As a second-generation Chinese growing up in Canada, this caused me a lot of internal conflicts. I often felt pulled in different directions and had no real sense of boundaries. I mostly found myself torn between what my parents wanted me to do and what I wanted. Since Chinese and Western cultures are so different, I still struggle with this sometimes as an adult. So, setting boundaries is a skill best learned early.

As you learn your boundaries and how to enforce them, you may experience some pushback from your friends and family. You should expect this since they are used to you acting a certain way. A good example of this was when a friend of mine had a celebration dinner at her parents' home. One guest took exception to her perfume, and an argument ensued. Her parents defended the guest and ignored her. As a result, she felt embarrassed and let down by her parents.

If you have ever felt let down by a loved one crossing your boundaries, you are not alone. Do you have people in your life who ignore your boundaries because they either don't know what they are or, as in my friend's case, don't care?

If so, you must be clear with your family and friends about which behaviors are acceptable and unacceptable. If they truly care about you, they will respect your boundaries just as you will respect theirs. Again, this is not easy. People do not like change because we are creatures of habit. However, I promise that if you consistently define your boundaries with your loved ones, they will eventually begin to understand and respect them.

Setting Boundaries with Family

Setting boundaries with your family can be difficult. Because most families have a set way of thinking and doing things, when one person begins to set boundaries, other family members may feel disrespected or threatened by the change in behavior.

Although it may be difficult and you may feel guilty, you must establish healthy boundaries for yourself. Nobody else is going to do it for you. Determining what boundaries to set and how to communicate them can be difficult and dependent on various factors. Consider the following example to demonstrate this point:

Let's say you work at the neighborhood supermarket after school and on weekends. You intend to save all your earnings to purchase the most recent iPhone. On the other hand, your parents are not thrilled with the idea. Instead, they want you to save your money for college. Should you give in to your parents' wishes or get that iPhone you've been eyeing for months?

Consider taking a stand if the iPhone is truly important to you. Following is an example of what you might say:

I've been wanting this iPhone for 15 months, and I now have a part-time job. I can save up my own money to buy it. In six months, I can save $1500. You've always taught me to pursue my dreams, and this is exactly what I want. There will be plenty of time for law school, and I believe that taking a gap year will allow me to save enough money for an iPhone of my choice as well as some for college.

However, before making a final decision, you should also consider other factors. In the preceding example, you should not follow your desire for an iPhone blindly. To balance things out, ask your parents why they are upset with you spending all of your money on a mobile phone. Although our parents may not always realize they are overstepping our boundaries, most act with our best interests at heart.

In the preceding example, one could argue that saving for college is more important than spending all of one's money on a smartphone. One major reason is that college is as a long-term investment in finding a better job, whereas a smartphone is not. A smartphone's value depreciates over time and will most likely need to be replaced every few years.

If you want to buy a $1500 iPhone with your parents' money, they have every right to refuse you. Why? It's their money, and iPhones aren't cheap. However, if you worked all summer to save up for an iPhone, you have a stronger case of getting one because it is your money.

On the other hand, if your parents suggest getting a cheaper smartphone for $500 and putting the extra $1000 towards your college tuition, that's a conversation worth having. As a result, you must balance your desires and emotions with theirs; it takes time and practice to learn how to do this.

Most importantly, listen to yourself and think about why you want what you want. Remember that only you have control over yourself!

Another example of parents infringing on their children's boundaries is pressuring them to pursue a specific major or career path. This is precisely what occurred to me.

Most Chinese parents want their children to be doctors, lawyers, or businesspeople because these jobs pay well and are well respected. When I was younger, however, I aspired to be an artist (not exactly a typical career for an Asian). You've probably heard the stereotype of the starving or struggling artist. These were concerns shared by my parents. Fortunately, they did not put too much pressure on me and simply wanted me to find a good job where I could be happy.

My Asian friend, on the other hand, was not so fortunate. She wanted to be a nurse when she was in high school. She wasn't as academic as she could have been because of personal issues. But because she wasn't doing well, the guidance counselor informed her parents that she had no chance of passing the exams required for admission to nursing school. As a result, her parents refused to pay for her exams, forcing her to drop out. After that, she was called "useless" and "hopeless" because she didn't finish high school. The irony is that she is now the only one of her siblings with a degree and a post-graduate degree. Even though she did not attend nursing school, she was able to succeed on her own.

Aside from emotional boundaries, physical boundaries are frequently crossed. My mother always barged into my room without knocking when I was a teenager. She used to go through my things and rearrange them even though they weren't hers. As a result, I would become irritated and tell her not to touch my belongings. In her mind, she had no idea that this was MY personal space. She assumed that because I was her son, she had a right to my belongings and didn't need to ask my permission.

When setting boundaries with family, you must anticipate certain things. First, prepare to face disappointment, disapproval, and pushback. Second, this is not a black and white process. Sometimes, you will be unsure where to draw the line yourself. However, with practice, you will learn when to be flexible and when to put your foot down when it comes to your boundaries.

Setting Boundaries with Friends

I kept to myself in high school because I was extremely shy and didn't know how to interact with others. However, as I began college, I made more friends and gained confidence. As you begin college and your career, I hope you choose friends who share your values and respect you.

But what do you do if you have a friend now who disregards your boundaries? What are your options?

Begin by telling your friend that you don't appreciate their behavior or how they treat you. Be specific and clear. The key is staying focused on the issue and avoiding personal attacks.

For example, if you don't like how they make comments about your weight, tell them. Inform them why you don't like it and what action you want to see taken to change it.

For example, *whenever you say I eat like I haven't eaten all day, I don't like it. I know you think you're just kidding, but it still hurts. I'd appreciate it if you could refrain from saying that.*

This demonstrates to your friend what actions they can change in the future. Remember, if someone is not consistently nice to you, they are not a true friend. Surrounding yourself with people who are kind and add value to your life is critical.

Everyone has the right to be treated with dignity. Remember that change is difficult, so it may take some time for your friend to change their behavior. But be persistent and consistent. Sooner or later, your friend will get if they are indeed a true friend.

What if a friend doesn't want to change?

If a friend truly cares about you, they will try to see your side and respect your boundaries. It's as simple as that. If not, it is time to rethink your relationship with them. Here are some questions to ask yourself when considering whether to keep a friendship or not.

- Do they genuinely try to respect my boundaries once I have communicated it to them?
- Do they apologize if they slip up?
- Is their undesirable behavior getting less over time?
- Is my friend willing to change?

If the answer to these questions is no, you might have to reexamine your friendship with them. If your friend continues to disrespect you, you can say:

I have already told you many times that I don't appreciate it when you do X. However, I feel you haven't tried to change or respect my boundaries. Although I appreciate you as a friend, I will need some space from our friendship. I hope you understand.

As you can see from the message above, you are being clear and upfront about your feelings toward your friend. Even though it might be hard to let them go, you must take care of yourself in the end.

Setting Boundaries Around Screen Time

In today's interconnected world, our phones, tablets, and laptops play a big role in our life. This can cause numerous negative effects on our mental health, such as isolation, anxiety, depression, low self-esteem, and fear of missing out (FOMO).

It's easy to spend countless hours on social media sites like Twitter, TikTok, and Facebook. And before you know it, it is already 1 am, and you haven't started your assignment yet.

Unfortunately, coffee and energy drinks have become the drinks of choice for many students to deal with lack of sleep. However, these drinks are full of caffeine, worsening your anxiety and irritability.[28 As a student, I often drank 4-5 cups of coffee daily to stay awake during my classes. Even though it helped, it wasn't healthy or sustainable.

So, how do you set screen time boundaries?

Firstly, you need to be willing and motivated to set this boundary. You need to be aware of the negative side effects of excessive screen time on you mentally and physically.

Secondly, set a realistic limit on the number of hours you spend in front of a screen. Once that limit is set, stick with it. As with any addictive behavior, this isn't going to be easy. You have to stay committed, and consistency is the key. Here are a few tools I recommend to get started:

- WasteNoTime – Blocks sites that waste your time.
- News Feed Eradicator – Replaces the news feed on your social media sites with an inspirational quote.
- BlockSite – Keeps you focused by blocking time-wasting sites.
- Stay Free – Tracks your screen time, and limits apps use.

If you are addicted to your gadget, realize that the initial phase will be challenging. However, I promise that it gets easier, and you will realize that the world is a bigger and more interesting place beyond your screen.

Setting Boundaries with Others

Besides setting boundaries with your family, friends, and mobile devices, our professional relationships are also important. Bosses or coworkers who overstep their boundaries are common, including expecting employees to work overtime without extra pay, treating junior employees poorly, bullying, office politics, etc.

Setting boundaries at the workplace can be challenging, especially if a supervisor or manager is the one causing conflict. If you want to bring up an issue at work, it is best to do so privately with the person. Avoid having these discussions in front of everyone. And remember, Human Resources personnel always help with these situations.

Keep these points in mind to make the process as smooth as possible.

- **Keep a neutral tone.** Don't be too harsh or too soft.
- **Be specific** about the issue and suggest what changes you would like to make. Focus on the problem, not the person. *"I want to talk to you about X. When you ask me to do X, I feel uncomfortable."*
- **Be clear and confident.** If you come across us unsure, they won't take you seriously.
- **Be firm and assertive** even if you are talking to your senior. Even though they may be your boss, that doesn't give them the right to disrespect your boundaries.
- **Be respectful.** This is especially important in a professional setting.
- **Be ready to face some resistance.** People don't like change, so don't take opposition personally.
- **Be consistent.** Realize that it may take more than one try to improve the situation. Don't give up!

Tip: If you want more tips on how you can effectively make your requests, do the GIVE exercise on page 65.

If you've expressed your concerns and the situation hasn't improved, consider looking for another job if possible. I understand that this may not be easy or an option for you, but remember that no job is worth sacrificing your mental or physical health.

Worksheet: Exploring Your Boundaries

If you're unsure what boundaries to set, the following worksheet will help you figure things out. It has prompts to help you understand where or with whom you would like to set boundaries.

Think about someone with whom you want to establish boundaries. _Example: I want to set boundaries with my brother. He keeps entering my room without knocking._	

What kind of boundary do you want to set?
Below are different kinds of boundaries. What kind of boundaries would you like to establish with this person? We have solved the first one about the above example.

Type of Boundary	Acceptable	Unacceptable
Physical Boundary	_My brother can enter my room after knocking if I give him the go-ahead._	_Barging into my room and invading my space without seeking my permission first._
Physical Boundary		
Emotional Boundary		

Financial Boundary		

How do you feel about setting this new boundary? Is it challenging for you? *Example: I struggled with staying resilient in setting this boundary because my brother would not take me seriously.*

How do you ensure that your boundary is respected? *Example: I will keep on repeating my request to my brother, and I will also start locking my door and refuse to engage with him if he continues to cross my boundaries.*

Worksheet: Setting Boundaries

As we learned in this chapter, boundaries are the limits we set for ourselves to develop healthy relationships. They teach us how to say no while keeping the respect of the relationship in place.

In this worksheet, please come up with responses to these practice questions as if you were going through them in real life. Read the situation, and think about how *you* would respond to it while setting your boundary.

*Situation	Setting Your Boundary
You must wake up for a very important school project at 6 am. It is 11:30 pm, and your friend is calling you to rant about an ongoing issue with her boyfriend.	*I understand you are feeling upset. I wish I could speak to you right now, but I have a super early day tomorrow. Let's talk about it tomorrow after class.*
Your sister asked you if you could babysit her kids for the weekend. You have made plans with your friends to go out over the weekend. You guys planned this two months ago, and you don't want to cancel.	
A friend keeps posting about everything you guys do on their social media. You don't like this and want your friend to stop.	

*Situation	Setting Your Boundary
A close friend has expressed their interest in dating you. You're not into that, but you don't want to ruin your friendship. You want to turn them down gently.	
You are walking your dog on the street when your neighbor comments on your weight and body size. You don't appreciate the personal remarks.	
Your mom/dad keeps yelling at you to do something (e.g., clean your room, take out the trash, watch your baby sister, etc.). It's stressing you out, and you want to tell your parent to just ask instead of shouting.	

Please feel free to write down additional situations and the boundaries you want to set for them in the spaces provided below.

*Situation	Setting Your Boundary

Chapter 11: Depression

"You don't have to struggle in silence. You can be unsilent. You can live well with a mental health condition as long as you open up to somebody about it."
-Demi Lovato

Today's teens and young adults are more depressed than ever before. According to Mental Health America, nearly 11% of youth today cope with *severe major depression*.[29] One of the reasons for this is that they are facing more pressure now at home and school than previous generations. There's also the very real fear of a bleak future. When COVID hit, it was estimated that 20.5% of adolescents globally displayed elevated levels of depression and anxiety.[30]

I talked to a friend about how we both had our struggles as kids, and it made me sad to hear my friend describe her experience with depression.

"At 14, my depression manifested in not being able to sleep. As a result, I was always grumpy and withdrawn. My parents thought I was just 'acting up', so they tried to 'discipline' me. I was unsupported and teased at home and bullied at school. Depression set in like a heavy fog. The only place I felt safe was with my church's youth group. There, I felt like I belonged, was loved, and was accepted."

Does this sound familiar? Even if you haven't been through the same things as her, I'm sure you know what it's like to feel sad, grumpy, angry, and withdrawn. Imagine not being helped or supported in any way by anyone. It's not surprising that she suffered from depression for a long time.

Understanding Depression

Depression is a common illness with physical, mental, and emotional consequences. When you are depressed, it is easy to lose interest in daily activities, activities that used to bring you joy, and life in general.

Depression Causes

A variety of factors causes depression. The number of changes in your life as an adolescent, all coming from different directions, may leave you feeling anxious, stressed, alone, and depressed.

For example, you could have problems at home, such as your parents not getting along or even discussing divorce. You don't feel like you belong at school and have difficulty getting along with others. To make matters worse, you're bullied on social media. This is causing you stress and anxiety, affecting your grades, and making your parents angry. You begin to believe that nothing is going right, and you may become depressed. And without anyone's support or guidance, this can quickly devolve into depression.

Depression Symptoms

Depression is not always easy to spot because some people hide it well. Unfortunately, too many people think that teens are just being dramatic or are in one of their 'moods', so depression may be swept under the rug. But following are some of the behavioral and emotional changes of someone experiencing depression.

Behavioral Changes
Keep an eye out for behavioral changes such as:

- Loss of energy and joy in life in general

- Insomnia or sleeping too much
- Appetite changes
- Use of alcohol or illegal drugs
- Nervousness or restlessness
- Slowing of thought, speech, or movement
- Sudden frequency of complaints
- Social isolation
- Poor school performance
- Poor attention to personal hygiene or how one looks
- Lashing out, exhibiting risky behavior
- Engaging in self-harm
- Planning or attempting to take one's life

Emotional Changes

Keep an eye out for emotional changes such as:

- Extreme sadness
- Extreme frustration or anger, even over little things
- Feelings of emptiness or hopelessness
- Loss of interest in activities they used to like
- Always arguing with family and friends
- Completely disengaging with family and friends
- Feelings of worthlessness or shame
- Excessive self-blame or self-criticism
- Extreme reassurance seeking and excessive sensitivity to failure or rejection
- Thoughts of self-harm or taking one's life

IMPORTANT: If you're noticing any of the symptoms above in yourself and yet adults dismiss you, don't accept it and stand for yourself. Be your own health advocate. Approach your parents. *I don't feel like myself and am not seeing good in many things and life i*, a teacher, a pastor, a guidance counselor, or anyone who can help and say, *"This is important. Please listen n general. Please help."*

DBT for Depression

As mentioned at the very start of this book, the basic principle of DBT is **Acceptance** and **Change**. Let's break this down further in the context of depression: it is *acceptance* (of your depression), *tolerance* (finding coping mechanisms to endure feelings of depression), and *change* (taking the necessary steps to get better).

The following worksheets are designed to help you deal with depression. We suggest that you do them in sequence whenever you're feeling depressed.

Worksheet: Radical Acceptance and Change

Here's an example to help you.

ACCEPTANCE:

Things are difficult.

I am depressed today.

I can't find joy.

I don't want to talk or see anyone.

Too many things going on... I find it hard to deal with all of them.

I am not okay.

WHAT YOU CAN SAY TO YOURSELF:

"I am sad and depressed right now. I'm not sure why but this is how I feel and it's real.

But I know things can be better so I'm going to help myself and ask for help too.

I am going to look forward to 'better' whatever that may be for me."

DESIRE TO CHANGE:

Things WILL get better.

A bad day is not a bad life.

There will be joy

I will take it ONE STEP at a time. That is all I need to do.

I deserve to be happy.

I am worthy of healing.

Your turn:

ACCEPTANCE: DESIRE TO CHANGE:

WHAT YOU CAN
SAY TO YOURSELF:

Worksheet: Body Scan (Mindfulness)

This Mindfulness exercise will help calm your nerves, focus your thoughts, and center your being.

1. Sit or lie down, whatever is most comfortable for you.

2. Close your eyes.

3. Do the Box Breathing exercise (page 72) for four cycles.

4. Starting with the top of your head, become aware of your scalp.

5. Notice any areas of tension. Breathe in and as you breathe out, soften and relax that part.

6. Next, become aware of your forehead.

7. Notice any areas of tension. Breathe in and as you breathe out, soften and relax that part.

8. Continue down until you've covered your whole body.

Worksheet: STOP (Distress Tolerance)

STOP is a DBT exercise that will help you take control of your emotions so that you don't act on them.

S top.
Stop! Freeze and don't do anything. Don't even move a muscle. Completely and physically freezing for a moment prevents you from doing what your emotions want you to do.

T ake a step back.
Remove yourself from the situation. Take a deep breath and continue to do so for as long as necessary until you are in control. Do not allow your emotions to guide your actions. We hardly ever need to make a split-second decision about anything, so give yourself time before deciding on anything.

O bserve.
Take note of what is going on within you and around you. Do this mindfully. That is, literally observe things as if you're making a list. An example of observing yourself: *I'm sitting. My heart feels heavy. My hands are clenched.*

An example of observing your surroundings: *The temperature control says it's 22°C here. People are running around. A kid is crying.*

What are you observing?

_____

_____

_____

_____

P roceed mindfully.

You've taken a break from your emotions, and now it's time to proceed mindfully. Ask yourself, "*What should I do to improve this situation?*" Example: *I'm having self-harming thoughts. I'm going to call a hotline right now to talk to someone.*

What do you want to do to proceed mindfully?

_____

_____

_____

_____

Worksheet: Opposite Action (Emotion Regulation)

When depressed, we should avoid acting on our urges (natural tendencies). This DBT exercise will assist you in NOT DOING what you are thinking or planning to do when you are depressed.

Emotion	Emotion-Driven Behavior *What you would normally want to do.*	Opposite Action *What you should do instead.*
Depression	*Self-isolate (not want to talk or see anyone).*	*Call a few friends and meet up with them.*
Depression		
Helplessness		
Sadness		
Unworthiness		
Shame		
Feel free to add other Emotions on the extra rows below.		

Conclusion

Our journey into learning about the various mental health issues that affect teens and young adults, as well as how to use DBT to improve and heal from these conditions, is about to end in this book. Please keep in mind, however, that overcoming mental health challenges is a lifelong journey.

To summarize, we discussed the following mental health issues:

- Anxiety, stress, and worry
- ADD/ADHD
- Phobias and Panic Disorders
- PTSD
- OCD and Compulsive Behaviors
- Eating Disorders
- Self-harm
- Boundaries
- Depression

We also talked about Dialectic Behavior Therapy (DBT) and its four skill modules:

- Mindfulness Skills
- Distress Tolerance (or Reality Acceptance) Skills
- Interpersonal Effectiveness Skills
- Emotion Regulation Skills

No matter how hard your situation is or how upset you are, there are always ways to get through it and feel better.

You are not alone on this journey. We all have our problems, but we are all in this together. When you realize this, you will feel a sense of belonging, and you can start practicing self-acceptance instead of self-criticism.

Remember that we are all different and can process things at different speeds and in different ways. The main goal is to be aware of your pain and any mental health issues you may have and then to try and use DBT to start your journey to healing.

Even though you may not completely heal from your mental health problems, there are certain things you can do now to help you deal with them better. Medication can help when needed, but it's also important to try some of the following:

- Eat a healthy, balanced diet.
- Improve the quality and quantity of your sleep.
- Exercise regularly.
- Listen to your body and give it rest when needed.
- Limit foods and drinks that harm your body (e.g., junk food, caffeine, processed food, high-sugar drinks, etc.)
- Avoid drugs and alcohol.
- Learn to accept yourself.
- Set specific and realistic goals.
- Surround yourself with high-energy, positive people.
- Be responsible for your mental health healing.

Life is hard, and it never fails to throw you curve balls. But it would be helpful if you're thankful for everything you have and enjoy every moment. Don't forget to be kind to yourself, and treat yourself like you would a loved one.

You embarked on this journey of self-development when you picked up this book. Thank you for picking this resource and investing your time in it.

If you or someone you know is in crisis, please seek help immediately. You can call 911, seek your local suicide hotline, or go to your local emergency room.

You may not realize it at times, but you bring so much value to life and this world. Keep shining!

"Do not let what you cannot do interfere with what you can do."
- John Wooden

Review Request

If you enjoyed this book or found it useful...

I'd like to ask you for a quick favor:

Please share your thoughts and leave a quick REVIEW. Your feedback matters and helps me make improvements to provide the best books possible.

Reviews are so helpful to both readers and authors, so any help would be greatly appreciated! You can leave a review here:

https://tinyurl.com/dbt-teens-review

Or by scanning the QR code below:

Also, please join my ARC team to get early access to my releases.

https://barretthuang.com/arc-team/

THANK YOU!

Further Reading

DBT Workbook for Adults

Develop Emotional Wellbeing with Practical Exercises for Managing Fear, Stress, Worry, Anxiety, Panic Attacks, Intrusive Thoughts & More

(Includes 12-Week Plan for Anxiety Relief)

Get it here:
https://tinyurl.com/dbtadult

Or by scanning the QR code below:

DBT Workbook For Kids:

Fun & Practical Dialectal Behavior Therapy Skills Training For Children

Help Kids Recognize Their Emotions, Manage Anxiety & Phobias, and Learn To Thrive!

Get it here:
https://tinyurl.com/dbtkids

Or by scanning the QR code below:

About the Author

Barrett Huang is an author and businessman. Barrett spent years discovering the best ways to manage his OCD, overcome his anxiety, and learn to embrace life. Through his writing, he hopes to share his knowledge with readers, empowering people of all backgrounds with the tools and strategies they need to improve their mental wellbeing and be happy and healthy.

When not writing or running his business, Barrett loves to spend his time studying. He has majored in psychology and completed the DBT skills certificate course by Dr. Marsha Linehan. Barrett's idol is Bruce Lee, who said, "The key to immortality is first living a life worth remembering."

Learn more about Barrett's books here:
https://barretthuang.com/

Glossary

Anxiety

A natural reaction to stress AND worry.

Attention Deficit Hyperactivity Disorder (ADHD)

A long-lasting disorder that affects a person's capacity to focus, sit still, and control behavior.

Cognitive Behavior Therapy (CBT)

A form of psychological treatment aims to reduce symptoms of various mental health conditions, primarily depression and anxiety disorders.

Depression

A condition characterized by a persistent feeling of sadness.

Dialectical Behavior Therapy (BDT)

A modified type of cognitive-behavior therapy that's been specially adapted for people who feel emotions intensely.

Eating Disorders

A mental health issue that causes unhealthy eating habits to develop.

Generalized Anxiety Disorder (GAD)

A condition characterized by persistent worrying or anxiety about several areas that are out of proportion to the impact of the events.

Obsessive-Compulsive Disorder (OCD)

A condition in which people have recurring, unwanted thoughts, ideas, or sensations (obsessions) that make them feel driven to do something repetitively (compulsions).

Panic Attack

A brief period of extreme fear that results in strong physical symptoms despite the absence of any real danger or apparent cause.

Panic Disorder

An anxiety disorder characterized by sudden and recurring bouts of great fear, which may go with physical symptoms such as chest pains, heart tremors, panting, vertigo, or gastrointestinal problems.

Phobia

Anxiety or aversion to something excessive or unjustified.

Post-Traumatic Stress Disorder (PTSD)

A disorder that progresses in some people after witnessing a shocking, frightening, or dangerous event.

Self-Harm

A condition wherein one wants to hurt one's self on purpose to relieve emotional pain.

Social Anxiety Disorder (SAD)

A condition characterized by an intense and persistent fear of being observed and judged by others.

Stress

The body's natural way of responding to external environmental changes or situations where we feel like we're being pushed beyond our limits.

Worry

A state of being where one is consumed by negative thoughts.

Index

References

1 World Health Organization. (n.d.). *Adolescent mental health*. World Health Organization. Retrieved July 7, 2022, from https://www.who.int/news-room/fact-sheets/detail/adolescent-mental-health

2 Bethune, S. (2019, January). *Gen Z more likely to report mental health concerns*. Monitor on Psychology. Retrieved July 7, 2022, from https://www.apa.org/monitor/2019/01/gen-z

3 U.S. Department of Health and Human Services. (n.d.). *Eating disorders*. National Institute of Mental Health. Retrieved July 7, 2022, from https://www.nimh.nih.gov/health/statistics/eating-disorders#part_2573

4 Muehlenkamp, J. J., Claes, L., Havertape, L., & Plener, P. L. (2012). International prevalence of adolescent non-suicidal self-injury and deliberate self-harm. *Child and Adolescent Psychiatry and Mental Health*, 6(1). https://doi.org/10.1186/1753-2000-6-10

5 *2020 mental health in America - youth data*. Mental Health America. (2020). Retrieved July 7, 2022, from https://mhanational.org/issues/2020/mental-health-america-youth-data

6 Linehan, M. (2021). *Building a Life Worth Living: A Memoir*. Random House.

7 American Psychological Association. (n.d.). *Teen stress rivals that of adults*. Monitor on Psychology. Retrieved July 7, 2022, from https://www.apa.org/monitor/2014/04/teen-stress

8 *17 remarkable career change statistics to know (2022)*. Apollo Technical LLC. (2022, March 24). Retrieved July 7, 2022, from https://www.apollotechnical.com/career-change-statistics/

9 McCarthy, C. (2019, November 20). *Anxiety in teens is rising: What's going on?* HealthyChildren.org. Retrieved July 7, 2022, from https://www.healthychildren.org/English/health-issues/conditions/emotional-problems/Pages/Anxiety-Disorders.aspx

10 Hofmann, S. G., Sawyer, A. T., Witt, A. A., & Oh, D. (2010). The effect of mindfulness-based therapy on anxiety and depression: A meta-analytic review. *Journal of Consulting and Clinical Psychology, 78*(2), 169–183. https://doi.org/10.1037/a0018555

11 Powell, A. (2018, August 27). *Harvard researchers study how mindfulness may change the brain in depressed patients.* Harvard Gazette. Retrieved July 7, 2022, from https://news.harvard.edu/gazette/story/2018/04/harvard-researchers-study-how-mindfulness-may-change-the-brain-in-depressed-patients/

12 American Psychological Association. (2019, October 30). *Mindfulness meditation: A research-proven way to reduce stress.* American Psychological Association. Retrieved July 7, 2022, from https://www.apa.org/topics/mindfulness/meditation

13 Mitchell, J. T., McIntyre, E. M., English, J. S., Dennis, M. F., Beckham, J. C., & Kollins, S. H. (2013). A pilot trial of mindfulness meditation training for ADHD in adulthood: Impact on core symptoms, executive functioning, and emotion dysregulation. *Journal of Attention Disorders, 21*(13), 1105–1120. https://doi.org/10.1177/1087054713513328

14 *Phobias.* Johns Hopkins Medicine. (n.d.). Retrieved July 7, 2022, from https://www.hopkinsmedicine.org/health/conditions-and-diseases/phobias

15 Bögels, S. M., Sijbers, G. F., & Voncken, M. (2006). Mindfulness and task concentration training for Social Phobia: A pilot study. *Journal of Cognitive Psychotherapy, 20*(1), 33–44. https://doi.org/10.1891/jcop.20.1.33

16 Carpenter, J. K., Sanford, J., & Hofmann, S. G. (2019). The effect of a brief mindfulness training on distress tolerance and stress reactivity. *Behavior Therapy, 50*(3), 630–645. https://doi.org/10.1016/j.beth.2018.10.003

17 *VA.gov: Veterans Affairs.* How Common is PTSD in Children and Teens? (2018, September 18). Retrieved July 7, 2022, from https://www.ptsd.va.gov/understand/common/common_children_teens.asp

18 Renoir, T., Hasebe, K., & Gray, L. (2013). Mind and body: How the health of the body impacts on Neuropsychiatry. *Frontiers in Pharmacology, 4.* https://doi.org/10.3389/fphar.2013.00158

19 Centers for Disease Control and Prevention. (2020, September 10). *Sleep in Middle and high school students.* Centers for Disease Control and Prevention. Retrieved July 7, 2022, from https://www.cdc.gov/healthyschools/features/students-sleep.htm

20 Cougle, J. R., Timpano, K. R., Fitch, K. E., & Hawkins, K. A. (2011). Distress tolerance and obsessions: An integrative analysis. *Depression and Anxiety, 28*(10), 906–914. https://doi.org/10.1002/da.20846

21 Rienecke, R. (2017). Family-based treatment of eating disorders in adolescents: Current insights. *Adolescent Health, Medicine and Therapeutics, Volume 8,* 69–79. https://doi.org/10.2147/ahmt.s115775

22 Calvete, E., Royuela-Colomer, E., & Maruottolo, C. (2022). Emotion dysregulation and mindfulness in non-suicidal self-injury. *Psychiatry Research, 314,* 114691. https://doi.org/10.1016/j.psychres.2022.114691

23 Yusainy, C., & Lawrence, C. (2014). Relating mindfulness and self-control to harm to the self and to others. *Personality and Individual Differences, 64,* 78–83. https://doi.org/10.1016/j.paid.2014.02.015

24 Brereton, A., & McGlinchey, E. (2019). Self-harm, emotion regulation, and experiential avoidance: A systematic review. *Archives of Suicide Research, 24*(sup1), 1–24. https://doi.org/10.1080/13811118.2018.1563575

25 Bratman, G. N., Hamilton, J. P., Hahn, K. S., Daily, G. C., & Gross, J. J. (2015). Nature experience reduces rumination and subgenual prefrontal cortex activation. *Proceedings of the National Academy of Sciences, 112*(28), 8567–8572. https://doi.org/10.1073/pnas.1510459112

26 Bakir-Demir, T., Berument, S. K., & Akkaya, S. (2021). Nature connectedness boosts the bright side of emotion regulation, which in turn reduces stress. *Journal of Environmental Psychology, 76,* 101642. https://doi.org/10.1016/j.jenvp.2021.101642

27 Thoma, M. V., La Marca, R., Brönnimann, R., Finkel, L., Ehlert, U., & Nater, U. M. (2013). The effect of music on the Human Stress Response. *PLoS ONE, 8*(8). https://doi.org/10.1371/journal.pone.0070156

28 Winston, A. P., Hardwick, E., & Jaberi, N. (2005). Neuropsychiatric effects of caffeine. *Advances in Psychiatric Treatment, 11*(6), 432–439. https://doi.org/10.1192/apt.11.6.432

29 *Youth Data 2022.* Mental Health America. (n.d.). Retrieved July 7, 2022, from https://www.mhanational.org/issues/2022/mental-health-america-youth-data

30 Racine, N., McArthur, B. A., Cooke, J. E., Eirich, R., Zhu, J., & Madigan, S. (2021). Global prevalence of depressive and anxiety symptoms in children

and adolescents during COVID-19. *JAMA Pediatrics, 175*(11), 1142. https://doi.org/10.1001/jamapediatrics.2021.2482

Made in the USA
Las Vegas, NV
30 August 2023

76829951R00105